Therapy for No One in Particular

The Autobiography of Just Some Guy

Christopher J. Paige

Green Heart Living Press

Therapy for No One in Particular: The Autobiography of Just Some guy

Copyright © 2022 Christopher J. Paige

All rights reserved. No part of this book may be used or reproduced by any means, graphic, electronic, or mechanical, including photocopying, recording, taping or by any information storage retrieval system without the written permission of the publisher, except in the case of brief quotations embodied in critical articles and reviews.

ISBN Paperback: 978-1-954493-15-5

Cover photo: Kristin Hornedo
Cover design: Teresa Hnat

This book is designed to provide information and motivation to our readers. It is sold with the understanding that the publisher is not engaged to render any type of psychological, legal, or any other kind of professional advice. The content of the book is the sole expression and opinion of its author, and not necessarily that of the publisher. No warranties or guarantees are expressed or implied by the publisher's choice to include any of the content in this volume. Neither the publisher nor the author shall be liable for any physical, psychological, emotional, financial, or commercial damages, including, but not limited to, special, incidental, consequential or other damages. Our views and rights are the same: You are responsible for your own choices, actions, and results.

Dedication

I dedicate this book to everyone that has supported me and everyone that opposed me in my life, because you all have collectively given me the balanced level of inspiration required to accomplish this undertaking.

Table of Contents

Introduction	7
Part I: Therapy for All Involved	13
Part II: Not My Cup of Tea	47
Part III: People Behaving Badly	71
Part IV: Just Some Guy's Survival Guide	119

Introduction

I wrote this book over 15 years ago as, well, therapy after watching my father slowly leave this world after a series of strokes. There are a lot of things that people don't think about on a regular basis that go into the writing process. I think that one of the most important things with any type of work of art is that there is a release and combination and closure for the artist and the viewer. Somehow, that has to be achieved over the interlacing of subjects and verbs, idioms and gerunds, participles and adjectives. With all of those structures crisscrossing hundreds of pages of writing, it's only logical that there has to be some type of Matrix where inspiration meets organization.

By a combination of happenstance, my editor Liz and I discussed removing one specific chapter of this book, and, weirdly enough, the major issue that was presented in the chapter was an ongoing battle in my life that has come to resolution. just recently. When I was creating the chapter in question, I was juggling phantasms of my past and present at that time and my future fears, and how close this chapter in question came in my life might have been too close for public consumption. It just seems prophetic to me that the chapter that had just been closed in my life was also the chapter that Liz thought might be a good idea to shift around or rework. I finally have words to express the joy that I feel now that this one chapter in my life, literally a chapter in my first full book, has come to a close. So, I am very appreciative that I have been able to be even here, meaning mentally present enough, to appreciate the value in this moment.

    I think that one of the most important things that I've learned how to do in my life is to edit. I have a natural ability for explaining things to people in various ways, using examples that I feel are apropos to them, or are palatable to a large group of people. Dance students of mine often say that they love my examples because I read somewhere that things that are taboo or comical are much easier to remember, so I would tend to make examples that are weird or bizarre in a comical sense. I spend a lot of my time teaching, so I guess that I am always in a space where I am poised to figure out what is the best way to communicate the information I need to relay. Communication is tough because everything can sound great in your head and the listener can think it sounds like Morse code. Also, since people don't normally have a sidebar about their conversations mid-conversation, you'll often not be able to pinpoint where discrepancies in communication occur, especially in situations where there's lots of excitement or fear.

    Working with an editor has taught me a lot as well. Fortunately, I've been able to work with someone who I trust implicitly, and that doesn't happen often in my world, but especially with my art. The experience of getting *Therapy for No One In Particular* out into the world has been so easy and it gives me pause every day to think that I've had this foot for 15 years and done nothing with it until now. However, I think that my ability to work with an editor is emblematic of my ability to accept what other

Introduction

people think about me with the intention of taking any valuable criticism with me and moving forward with grace. I also know that I wasn't ready to share my baby with the world.

 I probably agree with anyone that is reading this and thinks that it's been sort of a ramble, but, this is a perfect way to explain, in a sense, what life has been like since I wrote this book. The book started as just something I was thinking about in the hospital when my father was in his coma. It materialized into the first thing on my bucket list as an adult. There was a lot of space and time lost after the death of my father and consequently the death of my mother. The one thing that remains constant is that I've never stopped writing, even as I have expanded my artistry through singing, dancing, and other abilities and talents. I've never stopped understanding the abreaction involved in taking ideas out of your head and committing them to ink, and then sharing that ink with other people, and then having other people to help you to share your heartstrings and silver-lined dreams as tattoos etched by large machines onto some type of recycled tree or programmed characters to appear a digital screen. This book that has been sitting in my Gmail account for years has been sitting there because there was so much more that I needed to know about myself and life to be able to be ready to release this book.

 When I originally named this book, I wanted it to be called *Autobiography of Some Guy:* Therapy for No One in Particular. The order of this title was because I wanted to combine a weird title with my idea of everyday heroism, my concept that everyone has a moment in their life when they were someone's hero, even if they didn't mean to help someone or even if they are not aware how they saved the day. I thought that therapy sounded too clinical, worrying that it might be misconstrued as a self-help book.

Looking back, I've realized that writing this book *was* my therapy after my father died. I wasn't dealing with my feelings about his death as much as I was dealing with my feelings about life and moving forward. I didn't understand that I faced depression and how it would affect me, nor did I have the scope in my head of the pressures and tribulations that I might see afterwards. However, I managed, maintained and persevered, and then started to figure out how to effervesce past the froth that life can create around anything that you do.

I survived so many events that I believed would break me. I did find my faults, the cracks in my armor, but I learned that no matter what, my armor still worked, even when it might not have been completely whole. I learned to believe that I can, to love myself, to challenge myself, to expect the best from myself. I learned to forgive myself for my transgressions and to recover from their aftermath as well as use these moments as learning tools. I have had to learn to accept myself, my body, my mind, my skin, my flaws and best features. I'm still learning, but I can also see that my principles and methodology are essentially the same, minus the things that don't work. I've found love with my partner Anthony Colon. I've learned to love someone unconditionally in all seasons, and I've learned to accept another person's unconditional love. At the same time, I've learned that

Introduction

my talents and abilities are parts of me that need to be exercised daily and I am no good to anyone if I am not happy myself. I've learned to say what I need to say, although it is what I struggle with most. I have learned to try, and try harder, and pivot, and find ways to smile. I wrote this book for everyone, but now I can admit that it was for my own catharsis and forcing myself to be accountable to move forward in my journey. These ramblings are my own, for everyone's consumption. This is my therapy, and I am not "no one in particular." I am Just Some Guy Talking.

Part I

Therapy for All Involved

Just Some Guy Writing

Ever since I was a little kid, whenever I was down or happy or sad, with basically any strong or important display of emotion, I had to write it down. It could be something as simple as that I took a drink for the first time in my life, or it could be as weighty as just having lost my dad. Anything that requires a lot of feeling or thought from me is something that merits being recorded. I have done a lot of that recording over the past few years as I was going through my discovery period, and in retrospect, I found that there were very funny, very poignant pieces that I had written detailing different events and aspects of my life.

More and more, I realized that a lot of people say, "I should write a book about my life," but never do it. Meanwhile, people who read or heard these written recordings would tell me that I should write a book. I kept my writings and the idea of writing a book on the back burner on a low boil. After losing my father in March 2004, I decided that I no longer wanted to be one of those people that just says that they are going to do it. It became time for me to gather up all of those crazy, quirky takes on issues in my life and fuse them together into one collected Pandora's box.

When contemplating what to call my work, I went through various possibilities. For a while, "Ramblings of a Twenty-Something Year Old Man" was the working title. However, I realized that what was developing was a testament to my solidarity with the everyday person. That's the "some" part of the "some guy" concept. I also saw that this was my testimonial to my version of masculinity and maleness. That is the "guy" part of the concept. All of this growth and discovery was based on my life. Writing about my own life allowed me to loosely apply the term "autobiography" to this work. Thus, this is the autobiography of some guy. I mean, who am I to have an autobiography? I am not someone important to the world. I am not famous. However, I have a pretty interesting life for a regular guy, and thus this autobiography evolved.

Where did the therapy part come in? Who am I to give therapy to anyone? Well, I do know lots of little things, and I have learned a great deal. Besides this, writing is not for everyone, but it is such a treasure when you release yourself on paper. It is a physical manifestation of your thoughts and it is a way to move from crazy to creative effortlessly. This is therapy for you and me, connecting all of us together in reflection on our crazy lives. Or something like that.

I don't know who is going to read my book, so I don't know where or when catharsis may happen for each reader, or even if it will at all. It is not directed to one type of person or problem, just anyone that wants to read what I have to say. So, at best, it is definitely therapy for me, but, nonetheless, "therapy for no one in particular."

I don't claim to have the answers to everything. In fact, I have no answer for you or me on anything. I am not offering the fountain of youth or the Holy Grail. All I know is that I have a ton of craziness to offer to an already crazy world. All that I know is my life. All of these stories are true; the names were changed to protect the innocent.

Timelines

The chapters in this book don't follow a specific path of time through my life, and there is a reason for that. The way that things go in my life, there is no real one set timeline. Things just sort of happen, sporadically, and don't relate to one another. It's hard to connect them in time. It is easier to connect them by category. All of my thoughts on hygiene, through all of the years, can end up in the hygiene chapter, etc.

And, it's my autobiography. If there should be anything that I can choose to do my way in my own life, it should be how the story of my life so far is told. I think that is fair.

There are various chapters, and if you are like me, you will probably read out of order, getting first to the chapters whose titles catch your eye the most. If you are methodical, this book will drive you crazy, since there is really no method to it. I am just telling my story the best way that I know.

So, enjoy, and keep your psychologist's number handy, because this is one crazy little book.

Football

I have never been a man's man. I was never the captain of the basketball team, nor did I want to be.

I've never known much about football except that it reminded me of the futility of war. This brings me to this next story.

Football...

So there I was, maybe 12 or so, putzing around the house with not much to do. My relative came up with the bright idea that we should go play football. This relative is older than I, and so were his friends, so this was the first piece of discomfort. Now I was in that strange area of preteen life where I wanted acceptance as much as I was rejecting society and all that good stuff. So, I had to weigh the pros and cons of this proposition.

Pros:

I get to hang out with the older kids. (Not so interesting in my book, since all of my friends were older than me.)

If I went, then I wouldn't be in the house to do any chores. To a 12 year-old, this is the closest thing that we could get to a high.)

And last but not least, I would probably get the chance to eat at a fast food place and order what I wanted, or at least hang out at somebody's house for a while, prolonging that sad drive back home. (When you are 12, going back home is cause for a depression that very few people can understand.)

The Cons:

I hated football. (I don't love it now, but I wouldn't necessarily throw up or become violently disturbed if anyone asked me to play it.)

I *really* hated football. (To me, it was the last bastion of machismo in my life, and I refused to give in to its pervasive ardor and deceptive team spirit. One day, I planned to once and for all rid the world of its evil ways, but for now, I had to settle for loathing it, silently.)

I really *really* hated being around people that like football, especially events that glorified the game. (I have been to maybe one live football game, besides the ridiculous attempts at it in gym classes in school, and the one that you will read about here. I went to one because I won Homecoming King. That was only because one of the responsibilities of the crown (somehow I wrote that with a straight face) was to be announced at the Homecoming game. There is more of this in the chapter called — hold on to your seats — Homecoming King.)

The jury returned the verdict that I should go, despite the haunting feeling that this was a big mistake and that I may never be the same after this wretched experience. I was not so right, not so wrong.

It really wasn't as bad as it could have been, but that has to do with just my natural reaction as opposed to knowing anything about the game. When the ball was thrown to me, I ran, and knowing that there are 18,000 burly and somewhat ill-cultured men running behind you, thirsty for blood, the best thing to do is to run like fire. And I did. I actually surprised most people there because, except for my relative and his best friend, no one knew that I am pretty quick. I ended up dragging like four guys with me as I crossed the touchdown line.

As for the other parts of the game, trauma might be the best word to use. Someone told me to be nose guard. Immediate stop signs were raised in my head. Nose guard? I don't want to do anything requiring me to guard anyone else's nose, or my own. I reneged on this position, citing the obvious, "I don't know what that means." So the genius of the group suggests that while playing the game, I should observe the other nose guards to see what they were doing and do that. Now, forgive me if I am wrong, but what was I supposed to do in the meantime? I considered feigning a seizure to rescue me from this situation, but I feared more my parents' anger at using insurance unnecessarily. So I pretended to do something while everyone was busy doing whatever they were running around doing, until someone noticed that I was doing the equivalent of busy work on the football field. I had to do *something*, of course, this is football. I should have been grateful to be able to participate in America's pastime. What was I thinking?

So, I grabbed some guy who had the ball and threw him to the ground. Problem solved.

He argued with me that I had ripped his windbreaker. I retorted that he shouldn't have worn something that he didn't want ripped to a football game. This bit of male bravado that I exhibited salvaged the rest of my sappy performance in this game, and my touchdown actually propelled me to some type of respectable status. Moreover, the windbreaker incident became my new way out of future games — of course, I didn't want to repeat this incident, so I would just keep my anger out of the football arena.

I still hate football.

Bears and Squirrels

If there was a male counterpart to Jessica Simpson, as far as the silly things that someone can say, I think that I would be voted to be that person. I realized this when I remembered that I asked the Chicken of the Sea question of my mother one day when we were shopping. (For anyone that doesn't know, Jessica Simpson asked her husband on her show if Chicken of the Sea was really chicken or tuna.) I was much younger, but it still took a while to register that this was a play on words, and that there was not a type of chicken that lives in the sea.

Can you bite someone else's teeth?

This is a question that I came upon one day, just thinking. This is why it is dangerous to let someone with ADD think with wild abandon.

My school apparently recorded the question that I asked once as one of the weirdest questions that their information line ever received. Here's that story.

I was in a supermarket with two really close friends, Manny and Cinthia, and Cinthia picks up this package that had a drawn picture of a bear. The bear had like the hugest eyelashes ever. It struck me that it seemed a bit useless for a bear to have eyelashes. It's not like they have mascara. I don't think that bears would really need to wink their eyes at anyone. So I ask in my glory, "Do bears really have eyelashes?"

Manny gave me a look of disbelief and told me that yes, of course, bears have eyelashes. He reasoned that they had to have eyelashes to prevent things from getting in their eyes. I answered back that this is why they had eyelids, and I didn't see why they would need eyelashes. That seems so unnecessary for an animal that can eat me. I feel like this: If you can get into a bear's eye, more power to you. That's a pretty specific agenda that most people would never need to undertake, so to the organism or particle that can do that, rock on.

I asked him how he knew, and the fact that he could not tell me for certain that they had eyelashes fueled my quest. Would I ever know? Did anyone know? So, over a week's time, I asked a great number of people, some of them a bit disturbed by the urgency of my questioning, and I got mixed results. I even tried to find an answer on the internet but to no avail.

At the end of the week, I knew that I had to do something about this. I called the school information line, and prefaced my question with an earnest plea, asking the operator to not hang up on me, this was not a prank call, I really need to know if bears have eyelashes, and please connect me with someone that would know. The operator of the school line really did try to find an answer for me on the internet (he didn't put me on hold so I could hear him musing to himself as to where on the net to find the answer) and when this did not work, he connected me to a wildlife specialist in the university.

The secretary for the specialist agreed with me that this was a strange question, and laughed, and gave me the e-mail of the specialist since he was to be out of the office for a couple of days. I wrote to him and he wrote me back. I couldn't bear to tell him that this question had me obsessed for a week, so I told him that I had bet my friend on whether bears have eyelashes. His response was "Yes, Chris, bears do have eyelashes. I hope you won the bet."

Very interesting.

When I was four, I heard someone mention about the Constitution that it gave us the right to bear arms. As a very literal child, who did not yet know the dual meaning of "arms," I took this to mean that we Americans had the right to own the arms of bears. This was very disturbing to my 4-year old mind. I thought, why would someone want the arms of bears? Don't bears need their own arms? Why would I need the arm of a bear? Soon, I learned that the word "bare" meant exposed or without covering, and never having seen the Constitution to see how the words in the sentence are spelled, I somehow rationalized that this meant that the Constitution gave us the right to show our arms. This made sense to me because I reasoned that all the pictures of what I considered old times never really showed people much with t-shirts and tank tops, so I thought that maybe this was because they hadn't yet received the right to bare their arms.

Later I learned that "bear," not "bare" was the word in question, and that "arms" also meant weapons, so this to me now meant that we had the right to own the weapons of bears. Again, this was so bothersome to my little mind. Don't bears have the right to protect themselves? What about their rights? What about their protection? Well, I felt, at least they still have their arms on their body because that would really suck to not have arms and not have weapons either.

Fortunately, I never mentioned that to anyone, and everything sort of fell into place one day.

The squirrel is the other animal that has ravaged my life. It started when in third grade my class had to make original books for the academic fair. I chose to write about squirrels. This book was a classic and I really wish that I could find it. It had the history of different squirrels, written in my little, or rather, very big, third grade cursive. Along with that, there was a squirrel puzzle, squirrel mysteries (I was a regular squirrel Shakespeare), and more.

Apparently, years later, a deranged squirrel fan came to stalk me — in my house. This squirrel was stuck in between the floors of my house. That sounds worse than it really is. The squirrel found its way in through somehow and was trying to get out, but it was stuck between the floorboards. It had all the room to move about and run, as we could tell because his scurrying around on one quiet day is what alerted me to his presence.

I remember vividly that my fan must have gotten really tired of not being able to get my autograph, because he started making a hole in the floorboards so that he could get out. The thing is that he was making the hole beneath him, which meant that if he got through, he was going to fall on our floor. My mother decided that she was going to try to poke at the squirrel with a broom, to scare him. I left the house, with this comical idea in my head of the squirrel, falling onto my mom's head and his getting tangled in her hair. My imagination is dangerous, as this chapter demonstrates.

As an aside, two short animal stories:

Once there was a pit bull in our backyard. My mother called the animal cruelty people for assistance. They told her to catch the dog, put him in a cage and then they would come pick him up. She told them, in her five-foot way way, that if she could do all of that on her own, she wouldn't have called them for help.

Similarly, when the West Nile Virus first surfaced in our area, my friend's mom found one bird dead on her lawn one day and another the next. The disease control people told her to put the birds in a bag, and store them in her freezer until they came to pick them up.

I don't really have a commentary on that except to say that I don't see how that would prevent the spread of a disease to bring possibly diseased birds into your house and put them in the freezer next to your vanilla ice cream.

Losing My Father

My father died of a rare cancer, multiple myeloma, which is cancer that involves the blood plasma, and the degeneration of his body due to the ravages of that disease as well as diabetes and high blood pressure. In the last week of his life, he had a heart attack and two strokes that left him with only a third of his brain intact. I could not believe that a human could go through so much at the same time. There was no feasible way for him to recover from all of these things.

There is nothing worse than losing a parent, except, I would guess, losing a child. I don't have a child and I don't plan to have one, but until that unlikely incident, I will never know a worse pain. This is a pain that lingers. It's like one of those pains that no medicine can seem to reach, no matter what you take. It's something that I take with me everyday and it puts me to sleep at night. I don't know if I am taking this too deeply, or if there is a way to take a death too deeply. How are you supposed to take death? How are you supposed to react when someone that you love is alive one minute and not the next?

I didn't get along with my father a lot because we were very alike. The areas in which we differed were the areas that caused us our clashes. I guess this happens a lot in families. I can really say that nothing that we went through was anything traumatic or out of the ordinary. Of course, growing up, everything seems big in the moment that it happens. He and I had an argument about ketchup. Well, the topic was not ketchup, but the use of ketchup sparked the disagreement. How ridiculous, right, you say, but it seemed so important at the time.

My father was an interesting man. He liked nice cars and good clothes, and he never looked unkempt. That is why it was so hard to see him in a hospital bed, with wires and tubes hooked up everywhere that they could find a spot to insert something. That is why the image of him receiving dialysis, seeing all of his blood being filtered through a machine because his kidneys could not support.

These images are definitely hard to recall and even harder to understand that I have made it through that section of my life.

Losing him though has shown me so much in my life. It showed me for the first time that I knew that I loved my father. It showed me that everyone loves differently, and sometimes, you have to accept the way someone loves you, even if it is not the way that you imagined. It's better that someone loves you in their own way than not love you at all. I know now the importance of this statement.

I learned that most things about which I used to deliberate on a daily basis are basically meaningless. So much can happen within one day that your whole world is turned around. There is no time to spend doing things that you loathe when there are other things that you can be doing with your existence.

As I mentioned before, that is one of the reasons that I started working on finishing this book. As an English major, I have read so many books that are not meaningful to me, and that I doubt benefit the general populace. Why should my story not be available to the masses, when parts of it have humored so many? I wish that my father were here to see this progress in my life. It is a shame in one way, but amazing in another way, that this loss has made me so committed to living. I can't say that I am excited about living every day, or that I feel like I have a purpose every day. This had made me question the purpose of life a lot. However, one thing that is sure is that I know that I would never want to stop living.

Nothing in life will sober you more than sitting in your father's favorite chair with his ashes in a box in your hand.

Happy People Don't Have Bad Moods

I think that I am a moody person. I go through all of these moods each day. I get happy and then I get sad, and then I want to get in a truck and run people over, and then I want to jump around for hours for no reason. And it never makes sense to me. I will be in the middle of doing something that requires me to be really nice, like when I would work in the mall and have to deal with the dredges of society that dragged themselves through our doors to see what was on sale (not necessarily to buy anything), and then all of a sudden, my mood drops for no reason. My blood turns to vinegar and everything seems like the world is ending.

I have been like that all of my life. Psychologists have told me that this is somewhat a function of my ADD, having a high level of intelligence and being creative. I am always on a natural high, except when I am on a natural low. There is no even setting for me. It's like living on a roller coaster. It's fun and exciting, but when everything drops, it really drops.

This is certainly something that most of the people in this world endure. However, it is never allowed when you are what is considered to be a happy person. Somehow, because innately, you tend to be a little more outgoing and pleasant than the rest of the world, you are typecast with a perpetual smile on your face. People look to you for sunshine in their day as if the sun went on vacation.

Now it is not the worst thing in the world to be considered to be a happy person. However, there are those that take it to the extreme, as if it is your job to make their world a better place to be. God forbid that you are sick. That cannot happen. You are supposed to be there when they get sick to make them feel better.

It gets even better when you are in a bad mood or depressed. You can't be depressed. Happy people don't have bad moods. Happy people don't have bad days. A happy person has a permanent ray of sunshine that follows them wherever they go, regardless of the black clouds that are fighting to get over their heads.

So, instead of getting the support that you need

from people when you are down, here's what you get:

"What's gotten into you?

What's wrong with you?

You're not supposed to be sad.

You can't be like this.

Snap out of it."

Of course. You figured it out. It was my evil plan all along to make your day bad by deliberately making my own day bad so that I would make you less happy by being sad. Did it ever occur to the not-so-happy people that they bring constant sadness to the lives of happy people every day?

Happy people are the ones that get subjected to the constant banter of these not-so-happy people, complaining about their lives and being sad and depressed. Why is there not the necessary reciprocation when it comes to happy people? Why do we get to be the receptacle for all your garbage everyday? Why do we have to be the bellhops that carry your extra baggage when you check into the hotel of your next emotional nightmare?

Can you tell that people decided that I needed to talk to them, and then when I didn't want to, that there was obviously something wrong with me?

Can you tell that I have had a bad day?

Can't Sit Still

When I was little, I hated going to sleep. I always felt that I was going to miss something incredible or exciting. I felt like, why did the adults get to stay up later than me? Was that when, after all the little people were asleep, that all of the adults got together and danced and jumped around and played with our toys? Was there really cool stuff that came on TV that only grownups can understand? Sometimes, when I couldn't sleep, I would look out into the hallway or into the ceiling until everything started spinning. I always suspected a little bit of a conspiracy there.

As I got older, I learned that what I was missing was bad reruns of bad shows and the ever-riveting infomercials.

Right now, I don't want to go home, so I am on a bus that will take almost a half-hour to get anywhere and then I am going to my friend's house (my friend doesn't know this yet). This assumes that my friend is home and that he is not busy. If not, I am going to walk home, and then try something else.

Earlier today, I got to work early, an hour earlier than I was supposed to. This never ever happens. I really had a breakdown. (Good thing that I have an appointment with my psychologist tomorrow.) So I got on a bus and literally went in a circle (I got off the same place that where I boarded) to avoid having absolutely nothing to do. As long as I have my music, I am good.

Maybe it's the fear of being alone too long? No,

for me, I actually think that it is the fear of being bored. Boredom is scary. It leaves all of this unfilled space where things happen and things have to happen or else time will strangle the sanity out of your brain. And it is especially worse when you don't have money, or a TV. Then it is like voluntarily admitting yourself into an insane asylum with a permanent weekend pass.

I guess it is that, since I have no attention span, distractions are like my drugs. So to be out of distractions is like being out of a drug for an addict. Maybe somebody will start a fight or something will explode or something. Anything will do. As an aside, my friend was home, and was on his way out to a club. How fitting.

Walking and Driving While Dark

This section bothers me that I have to write it but at the same time, the more that people know that things like this happen daily might one day make a difference. I couldn't document a story of my life without including at least a bare bones account of my run-ins with the law.

- I was walking down the street to the bus stop in California and got stopped there twice by policemen, saying that I fit the description of some guy who had passed off a bad check at the bank. I have never seen such a search for someone that passed off a bad check, although in truth, I can't say that I haven't either. Regardless, after the second time of showing them my ID and sitting on the sidewalk like a common criminal for them to find out twice that I was not the guy, the police apologized to me and then said that they should give me $5 for my trouble.

- I was followed for 20 minutes down the same road, a road that changes speed limit five times, and anyone that is not from the area would not know that. Fortunately, I did, since I traveled every day to work via this road. When the cop finally pulled me over, I asked him why he had stopped me. He told me that he wanted to make sure that the right people were in his town. I told him that in that case, this wrong person was about to leave his town.

- I got two tickets due to Identity Theft (someone used my name when stopped by the police). One time that this happened, I was in California when the ticket was issued and the other time one happened when I was an hour away at work. For the latter ticket, the person's physical description was of someone 60 pounds lighter than I, with green eyes and an inch shorter than me. The cop who issued me the ticket was present when I was pointing all of this out to the prosecutor, and the cop says, "Oh, I should have caught on to that." Well, I wished that he had caught on to it before I had to miss time from work and find some town that I have never heard of before.

- I was driving in a lily-white town with a white

girl at night, which is always just asking for trouble. I was stopped by a policeman of course. Bravely, I asked the cop why he had stopped me. He told me that I was speeding. I told him that this wouldn't make any sense because I was lost in a town that I did not know so if anything, I was going too slowly. Then he tried to tell me that he stopped me because I did not have my seat belt on. I let him know that I had taken it off so that I could get my wallet out of my bookbag in the backseat. Then he told me that my tail light was out. This I could not argue, not because I knew it to be true, but because I could not get out of the car and prove it false at the same time without incurring a beatdown.

It happens to every man of color. It just sucks when it happens to you.

Step-Grandfather

I wonder if the word step-grandfather exists.

I wrote the word "stepgrandfather" in a composition one time and Microsoft Word told me that this was not a word. I found that really odd because I would think that it does. I mean, if a step-father can have a stepchild, would that child not then be a step-grandchild that has a step-grandfather? I think that it might be because it is assumed by that time, if the family is still close once that child is born, you can just call that person grandfather.

Well, for me, I think that it is an important term. I had a grandfather and a step-grandfather. Now the odd thing is that the step-grandfather was the best example of a grandfather that I have known. However, I didn't really know my biological grandfather until years after my birth. This completely altered my life. To acknowledge the time that I lost, and the exact relationship that we legally had, I referred to my father's stepfather as my step-grandfather. Some people thought that this was mean or disrespectful, but I thought, *wasn't it disrespectful to hide my grandfather's existence from me?*

Families, especially extended family, create unnecessary drama to replace the awkwardness of the revelation of truth. I don't want to linger on this topic, but it is definitely one that requires exploration if you are to know my life.

I believe that family is not determined by blood but by performance. This is something that I live by. There are relatives that should relinquish that title because they serve no purpose to your family except being a constant source of pain and discouragement. There are friends that, though not blood relatives, would bleed for you, cry with you, take care of you, be at the hospital with you at any time you might need it, and at no cost except that you continue the relationship. It's funny how sometimes you find family in your friends. Fortunately for me, I have also had the benefit of having family, like my mother, father, and sister that have performed as family should.

There are people who have been there with me through the ups and downs of the last three years like only families can. They accept me with all my quirks, just like my own mother and sister. They laugh at my silly jokes, feed me when I come to visit, and make me forget that I have so many other reasons to cry. They reinforce my faith in love and life and always fill my heart whenever I am around them.

When pondering who to dedicate this book to, I was going to list everyone by name and write something nice to them. But then there was the problem of who goes first, what if I forget someone, and so much else. So, instead, I leave everyone with this idea:

I dedicate this book to everyone that has supported me and everyone that opposed me in my life, because you all have collectively given me the balanced level of inspiration required to accomplish this undertaking.

Mints

My book would definitely be incomplete if I did not mention my fetish for mints.

Anyone who knows me knows that I usually have mints on me, and not just any mints. Forget about your Altoids, your spearmint gum, your Tic Tacs. We are talking about those 5-cent jaw-popper peppermints. You know exactly what I am talking about. These are the ones that make you look like you have the mumps when you put them on the side of your mouth. These are the ones over which you must salivate at least for five minutes before you can return to talking or anything else that requires the movement of your mouth.

I think that I would dissolve into nothing if there were no more mints in the world.

There is something wrong in this world when we don't have time for mints. Mints are the things that make me tick. Other people have other little things about them that define and identify them. I am saying now that if I were ever to be in a coma, I would like to request mint flavored IV's. I love mints. I have talked before about how I like soda, but nothing compared to my love for mints. I would walk for 10 minutes on a bad ankle on a rainy day to go to this one location where they sell those 5-cent gumball size peppermints. This is not a conjecture — this actually happened.

I am not sure when it started, but it had something to do with the fact that I always like to have pleasant smells in my vicinity. You could be as attractive as you want, have as much money as possible, and be the best person the world has to offer, but if you have bad breath or a foul odor, you are a pile of rhinoceros poop to me. Also, when I was younger, I loved sour cream and onion potato chips and garlic, so mints were not just something I liked – they were necessary for my existence in the social sphere.

Good breath has always been something in which I have believed. Seriously, I think that it should be against the law to have bad breath. No one should be allowed to leave the house without fresh vapor exuding from their mouth. I sometimes wonder If people sometimes deliberately don't take care of their breath so as to aggravate people or make people not talk to them. Although this is not the worst idea in the world, it still requires a conscious effort to have unpleasant air come forth from your mouth.

As far as name brands, I have tried them all. I have had a pack of every mint known to man. I am convinced, though, that these 5-cent, no-name jaw-busting mints are the best kind. For 5 cents, you can get the very best in breath fresheners to alleviate the scent of your Chinese food or your onion and chives bagel.

I have literally taken walks at 1 AM to go to a little store that sells these mints. It doesn't matter the length of the journey. What is important is having peppermint in my mouth.

I think that if this gets any worse, I may have to go to Peppermint Anonymous...

Speaking in Tongues

I spoke Chinese at 7.

I spoke Latin at 11.

I spoke French at 14.

I spoke Spanish fluently at 23.

Who does that?

I have always been exposed to different languages. My name is a mixture of Greek, Hebrew, and French, so I guess it started from there. I remember that as a child, my father would speak a little Italian and Spanish to me. I was always exposed to Spanish, both written and spoken, from a young age. Most of it registered, although I never felt really comfortable speaking the language until a few years ago when I decided to stop being afraid of messing up.

This mixture of languages has always made me feel like I need to study a language every day of my life. It attacks me all the time. For instance, many times, when I start reading a book, I start from the back page as if I were reading in Chinese. A better example is that I was at the bus stop one day and I asked this man for the time. I asked him three times and he never answered me. Sensing the frustration on my face, he asked me, "Do you speak English?"

This is when I realized that I had been speaking to him in French the whole time.

I think that being in a multilingual environment has definitely benefited me. I usually think of various ways to say the same thing, because I know that sometimes things make sense in a different way in a different language. It has also served to make me crazy. There are many times when I can't think of what to say, because there are so many different languages in which to say it. The worst thing that the world could have done is give someone like me, who loves to talk, the ability to speak more than one language.

Deficit of Attention

If you read the chapter about Happy People, you will understand a little bit about what my life has been like. I have been like that all of my life. Psychologists have told me that this is somewhat a function of my ADD, having a high level of intelligence and being creative. I am always on a natural high, except when I am on a natural low. There is no even setting for me. It's like living on a roller coaster. It's fun and exciting, but when everything drops, it really drops.

ADD is just another aspect of my day-to-day issue.

Imagine for a moment a huge traffic jam. In New York. Rush hour. Friday. When the president is in town.

Imagine the Autobahn.

Think of a beehive.

Splice those three images together and you have a basic example of what happens in my brain every day.

It is hard for me to play pool because all of the colors and patterns on the balls distract me. Those pictures that you are supposed to look at for 30 seconds and then you see the image — I have never once seen the image. My mind is too busy being occupied by those thousands of little dots that I can't focus back on the real picture.

Information overload is something that happens

to people that have ADD or ADHD. All of that mental traffic starts flowing and before you know it, there is a freeway going on in my cerebrum. It gets so bad that sometimes I have to sit down. It's like someone is hanging on my head...not heavily at first, but then it drags you down.

A good way to illustrate what happens with me is this. I was with a friend and she was a rabbit and she directed my attention toward it. My response — "I have to go to the gym." That was honestly my first response. This is why: Rabbits jump. Jumping made me think of jumping rope. That I had not jumped rope in a long time reminded me that I needed to go to the gym. Therefore, the rabbit made me realize that I should go to the gym.

Imagine living like that everyday.

It's not a problem. It is a learning and processing difference.

I always had the classic signs, but most of my teachers must have picked up on the fact that I was really bright and that with pushing, I could finish my work. The key here was pushing. If I were assigned 10 questions, I would do five. I could never complete anything. Cleaning my room was and still is as painful as removing my own intestine with a dull butter knife without anesthesia would be. My wardrobe has a lot of the same color in it, because I get distracted with lots of different patterns. You can't imagine how happy I was to see the monochrome look become stylish.

I forget my thoughts all the time. I have to take

paper everywhere I go like I have amnesia so that I can write down things that I need to know. This is useful, especially when I move from room to room and forget what I am doing in the first place. I have to do the crossword puzzle in class so that the teacher is my distraction and thus I end up paying attention to the teacher.

There are lots of other things that I do to cope with this, and I could probably explain ADD much better right now, but I am distracted by the need to write this chapter.

I tried to write this chapter so many times, but I lost focus.

Mighty Mouse is a Lie

I was really afraid of Mighty Mouse when I was young.

I had gone to a funeral of some relative who had died of a heart attack. This was my first time at a funeral, and I conveniently had an ear infection. I say it was convenient because I really did not know this relative, but the loud sounds of music hurt my ears so much that I could not help but cry. So it appeared as if I was crying about this loss, when in actuality, I was crying about the throbbing headache that was attacking my life. Anyway, the last song that was played reminded me of the Mighty Mouse theme song. (I realized that as an adult. Knowing this a long time ago would have helped a lot.)

So, you can imagine that every time that I heard the Mighty Mouse theme song, I would cry. I think in my head, these people don't realize that Mighty Mouse is a lie. He is the harbinger of death. He is not coming to save the day; he is coming to place everyone under his spell of benevolence so that he can then whisk them off to the land of death.

This is a short but necessary chapter, explaining how my indecently analytical nature has been plaguing the world since my birth.

A King without a Crown

I was Homecoming King.

Sometimes I still can't believe it. Not in the sense that the idea of my being Homecoming King was impossible or incredulous. It's more that I am not someone that has ever really been interested in these types of things. I have arduously avoided fads for most of my life. I have always been a nonconformist in most senses. Homecoming King seems to me to be one of the foremost symbols of conformity. It's like apple pie and baseball, an American tradition. There are people in small towns in this country who at 40 years old, probably still dust off their homecoming crown and reminisce on the day that they outshone everyone else that was running against them.

What is the accomplishment of Homecoming King?

It's not like you won Class President. It is not like

your science project was voted best-in-show. It's not like winning a race, or scoring high on a test, or even just the satisfaction of handing your work in on time.

All it means is that people liked you more than they liked some other slug. It's like being Miss America. As I mention in the football chapter, you have the responsibility of representing the school at various functions. As Homecoming King, I had to represent the school at Hispanic Culture Month, Black History Month, International Culture Month (or whatever it was called, it was in April, which is actually Asian American Culture Month), and more.

It was kind of fun, as I love to be in the spotlight, because that is the pinnacle of modesty. I feel like I am doing a community service, by showing how great humankind can be, taking attention away from the ugly and unimportant. (Ok, I am really kidding. I actually think that this is the pinnacle of selflessness.)

(Ok, I am really *really* kidding.)

Not that I am planning to relinquish my crown, but I hardly think that is a fair statement. I am not sure what statement my crown was. First, I was up against all of these guys from the football team. I was thinking that they would divide the votes enough that I could use the leverage that I had of knowing a lot of the not so popular people in the school to win. This is not what happened. There was some technicality where Homecoming King had to have a certain GPA. I don't know if this was because the committee reviewing the candidates took pity on me, and realized that this was the only way that I could win, but this measure eliminated all but two of us.

The other candidate was and still is one of my best friends.

I campaigned as if I was running for president of the world. I visited each classroom. I campaigned in Spanish. I would have relearned Chinese (which I learned from ages 7-12) if it was necessary. It could have been that I just knew more people outside of my immediate class than my friend, or that my campaigning actually worked, but I won. The ceremony was horrendous. All high school ceremonies for anything are supposed to be nothing but horrendous. The horror of the ceremony was not the ceremony itself. It was the lack of a crown.

Oh, don't get me wrong. There was a crown. I just never got it.

The crown was placed on top of this huge chair type contraption that was supposed to be the throne. As soon as I sat down, I was told not to move because the crowns were precariously placed in such a manner that a slight movement could send it crashing down on our heads.

Obviously, this meant that we were going to be crowned in a figurative sense, as in, just receiving the accolade.

However, I really just wanted the crown.

The whole point of all of that campaigning and extra effort was not so that I could receive some title. I could care less about that. I really wanted the crown. Who wouldn't want to have a crown in their closet, so that when you are looking back through your yearbook in college or grad school or with your children, you can pull out this gold foiled faux rubied, amethyst jeweled almost hexagon thing from the attic and say, "I was homecoming king." There is a certain ridiculous pride that this statement carries. Almost inexplicably so.

Winning this has not impacted anything in my life. Not one blasted thing. However, it is always a conversation starter. And you know, somewhere deep inside, no matter how long I am alive, when I reflect on high school with fellow classmates, I can proudly throw in something about my glorious reign and gloat for a minute that I won the vote that means nothing, but that everyone wants to win.

This is why it is most important to understand that we did not even get to *touch* the crown. In retrospect, maybe I should have made it fall on me, just so that I could touch it *once*. They gave me a scepter, but after the ceremony, I was informed that it was tradition (or rather the dictates of budget cuts) for the school to keep the crown and the scepter. The only thing that I retained for my own was the sash, and honestly, no self-respecting man is going to pull a homecoming sash out of his closet without raising questions about when the rest of him will come out of the closet. So, I had a successful, untarnished reign, without scandal, but sadly, my only regret is that I did not fight for my crown.

Maybe when I get to law school, I can run for homecoming intern or something like that.

Give me a break and let me dream.

Part II

Not My Cup of Tea

Guys

Black or white, tall or skinny, weird or normal, there are some things that I have realized that all guys have in common or do similarly. It is an undeniable fact. I have tried to convince myself that I am the anomaly. I *am* an anomaly in many ways, but not in the way that I always thought. I have always been a nonconformist for most of my life.

I was not one of those guys that ran out to go play football with all of the other guys. I was the one inside, doing my work, wondering when their game was going to end so they could finally shut up. I never knew when the Super Bowl was. I hardly know now, and that is only because I watch the halftime show. Even though my father and brother had weightlifting as a pastime, the only weight that I wanted to lift was my book bag.

Trust me, I did not grow up envying the popular kids, crying in my room, praying that my fairy godmother would rescue me from my dismal dungeon of nothingness. I always have managed to rise to some level of social stature in whatever environment I am in. What that babble means is that I don't remember not being popular. I was not one of the jocks, and was never one of the pretty boys, since I was always a heavyset kid. I guess because I inherited a good mix of charm, a kind of "if-he-was-thinner-I'd-go-out-with-him" good looks, and intelligence. (If that wasn't self-aggrandizing, I don't know what is.) I never had too many problems in the popularity department. Yet still, I think it was because I was the affable weird kid, the dude that likes the arts, and because I am a good listener that people have been drawn to me.

I still never felt any kind of sameness with the other guys. It's funny when I think about it now because I almost reveled in the fact that I didn't have anything in common with some of these people. However, there is a point that you reach when you realize that there is some solace in commonality. This, combined with the realization that nonconformity is not always the best idea, forced me to realize that in some way, I *did* want to be one of the guys.

The problem is that for most of my life, I didn't like men. What I mean by that is that I did not get along with other guys. I realized that it didn't matter if the guys were 5 or 95. I didn't really like talking to guys in my age group. I rebuffed any instruction given to me by male bosses when female bosses could give me the same instruction and it would not bother me.

At a vantage point a couple of years ago, I acknowledged to myself that other guys really weren't my cup of tea. I had a very aloof attitude to most other males. I would look at them in their t-shirts and sweatpants, beer guzzling, foul-mouthed, farting and burping, chasing women, and think, is this how I want to be viewed? Is this the group into which I want to be lumped? Not really. So where was I going to go? The last guy that would ever be put on the Man Show now wants to have male bonding. This was like Frasier trying to go play basketball in the hood. I felt a bit out of place, but one thing that I have learned is that the best way to do something is just to do it.

As I opened up and became a little friendlier to my brethren testicle owners, I realized that maybe, just maybe, I was not the complete alien in this world that I considered myself to be. For instance, I always thought that I was the only guy in the world that likes to just be able to sit around in his boxers and do nothing, just because I can. My less-than-professional survey has told me that, yes, this is a universal fact. The more and more that I have surveyed, the more that I have realized that I am not alone in this world, in the male sense of things. I *did* actually like to watch and play sports. I just didn't like people telling me that I had to play this, or that I couldn't like that. The older you get, the more people accept that tennis is not a sport just for girls, and I have received less strange looks from making the admission that that is one of the only sports that I like.

Now, I still don't get into the whole farting thing, although I have learned how to burp in front of my male compadres. I've been to a bar at happy hour no less, I have taken shots at a party, I have lived in a party house, I've thrown up from being drunk (once), and lots of other crazy rites of passage type things that you would expect a classic American male to experience. And, honestly, I have had a good time.

At the same time, I realized that the best way for me to be was to be me. The more that I have not tried to fit in, the more that the way that I am has opened up more doors for me, and more circles of friends have opened their doors to me. So now I know that other guys are ok, and so am I.

Defense

Life is sometimes like basketball to me. We have already established how I feel about sports, but here's the idea. Life requires you to be on your toes, ready to protect yourself from people's comments and actions. You also have to take it to the line as it were, and prove yourself. Other players take the position of just forging ahead through rough territory instead of staying in one place and defending.

I am tired of defending ideas and people. I find that I spend a lot of time debating things that are not of real concern. I don't like when my friends don't like another one of my friends. That kind of situation will see me arguing as if I am in court for the valor of this person. What do I really need to care about that for?

I do that with songs that I like, programs I like, stars I like — in general, with things I like. I guess because I have always been very independent, having a group of friends thrusts me into a situation where people don't have as set opinions as I do. I am also that way with my opinions and my level of comfort. I always feel like I have to defend these points, instead of being like the rest of humankind and just being sure about my feelings and learning not to relent.

For instance, one night, the guys wanted to go play basketball. I thought, well, ok, normally I would try to find some way out of this, but it was the three-month anniversary of my father's death, and I really didn't want to be by myself. However, even the threat of loneliness on this day was not enough to make me want to play basketball. Fortunately, I had three saving graces on my side to prevent me from getting to the core of the issue, that I really don't like anything about basketball (except for watching a live game of it, which requires no proximity to sweaty people grunting things that are only spoken in the course of a basketball game).

1. I was still recovering from a recent ankle injury, so I really shouldn't be doing anything truly strenuous.

2. I had on boots, which, especially for someone that doesn't play basketball, is probably not advisable. (I don't know about the veracity of that, but I figured that either way, sneakers would be more advisable.)

3. I wear size 13, and most of my friends have smaller feet than I, which means that no one would have size 13 sneakers to let me borrow.

The push was for me to play basketball though. I think, though, that once I eloquently explained that I was just going to watch (*"I'm not playing!!!"*), things were not so bad.

Until I mentioned that I don't play basketball.

This slight comment turned into one of those jaw dropping moments that happen in movies, like when the precious, ancient vase is dropping to the floor as someone dives to catch it, yelling "No-o-o-o-oo-o."

I was imagining that this was going to be the moment that Captain Testosterone was going to come and save the day, infuse me with the gene that I definitely missed, the gene that every guy but me received, the one that allows them to cancel wedding plans and quit jobs before they would miss a basketball game on TV. I even left the door unlocked, but sadly, he never showed up.

So I found myself where I find myself many a time, explaining away why I don't like to play the evil game. While I do like basketball more than other sports, agreeing to play it would still require my life being threatened. Not that I have ever heard of someone having to play because their life depended on it, but that is how serious it would have to be to see me dribbling a ball.

Just take the word dribble. What kind of a word is that? Dribble. It's like drizzle and quibble, which are two things that I think of when I consider basketball.

Drizzle because of all the sweat that happens playing basketball. It just always seems like people that play basketball are always drenched. I get sweaty just thinking about that much activity. And it's not like I don't exercise. I run and walk and do all sorts of calisthenics every day. I am not afraid of sweating, but basketball seems like it requires undue perspiration, and I am not one for the wet t-shirt look.

Quibble because it seems like basketball, especially street basketball, has four thousand different rules, that all differ wherever you may go. Every line and half circle means something different, and the points are different, and I just get frustrated. Just when you think that you have mastered the game, Joe from down the street plays a game with you and you find out that all the rules that you know are wrong in his book. That is why I don't play basketball anymore. Too much red tape for something that is supposed to be fun.

However, it's just a part of who I am as a person. I remember that once I actually admitted to someone that I was arguing with them just literally for the sake of argument. I wanted to see how long I could go on in the conversation without relenting or wanting to give in.

This is why I plan to go to law school and never, fortunately, to be a basketball star.

The Bermuda Triangle of Summer

I really need to get out of the city, move, do something different. I feel like I am being suffocated by seeing the same people in the same places doing the same things. Every event that I attend is put on by the same few people and is attended by the same few people. How many times in one day can you say hello to the same person without wanting to destroy them? That is the game that I play each day. Granted, most of the people to whom I refer are friends of mine, and it is wonderful to be able to work and interact with your friends on a regular basis, but I feel like that is all that I do.

I feel like I need another identity. It is summer right now, and I feel like I should not be running into the same people on a daily basis. However, the same people that have been with me throughout the whole year are practically on my shoulder right now, breathing the same breaths as I at the same time. This is as close as I can feel to understanding the life of a conjoined twin.

I want to be able to look around one day and see no one that I know, and not have anyone put me through a talk show. I just want to have my space. The bad thing about all of this is that it is no one's fault. I can't walk up to my friend and say, "Could you pretend like you don't know me for maybe two to three days or even weeks? I need to get myself together."

Especially in summer, you run into the Bermuda friend triangle. This is when either your friends disappear for the summer, or you disappear into the same group of friends and all of you are stuck together like there is no escape. This all may sound very misanthropic, but let's face it. Everyone likes to have their own time. Everyone likes to be able to just hear the sound of his or her own heartbeat without any interruption from anyone else. Sometimes, I think I understand how celebrities feel because here on this campus, I know lots of people; it seems like since I am a social person, I am never allowed my quiet time. People invite me places because I dance or I am social, like I am a jukebox that you just drop a coin into and it plays a song for you.

I guess that's why I can't stand the computer center. It is even worse than during the semester when you really need to get something done, and it seems like everyone wants to sit next to you and have the only conversation. If I am telling you that I have a paper due in two hours, then it might not be terribly time-efficient to tell me about how depressed you are from running into your ex RIGHT NOW. I would be glad to talk about that later, much later, when I can actually focus on the words coming out of your mouth.

The summer is a little worse. Since what I am doing is working on my book, that translates into people's heads as a frivolous activity that requires no attention or focus. They can see that I am sitting there with an unfinished chapter in front of me, and I have told people that my goal is to finish a chapter a day, which is not terribly unreasonable, but yet, I still need to hear about the trivialities of their world.

It is a little more bearable when this happens with different people. However, when it is the same crew, it's like repeatedly catching the same rerun of a show that you like. It wears you down, like the Macarena.

Summer has always been a boring time in this area. It is bad enough that being car-less in New Jersey is tough during the year. At least during the semesters, there are people around with cars, or people that might be going in the same direction as you. No, during the summer, there is no salvation. You are stuck here, day in and day out. It seems like walking around the block is my entertainment these days. Unlike other people that are dying to just stay at home and bask in air conditioning, I want to go, travel, and explore. I just don't have a way to do that.

Sometimes, when I was a teenager, my cousin and I would go and drive for hours, going nowhere, just around the block fifty times because there really is nothing to do around here. There were countless nights like those. Or we would go to the mall with money to put gas in the car and to eat, but that's about it. Not trying to buy clothes, we were just in the mall to laugh at the crazy things that happen in the mall. We would watch the mallrats, and the wannabe thugs from well-to-do families that went to the mall to try to be harder than the other crew of wannabes, and older women wearing their teenager's clothing to try to appeal to the young guys that work at the mall.

That seems so interesting and alluring right now, as I contemplate how I will try to numb myself into sleep today from the lack of excitement that this day has caused. The problem is that everyone around here is suffering similarly, but then when we see each other, we really don't have anything to say or to talk about. How many times can I tell you that this place is boring? It just is. There's nothing else to say about it.

So that's what happens. You either sink into the same group of friends, or you find a summer group that you will never hang out with again, or you go off on your own, but it seems inescapable until September comes around again.

A classic example of this summer boredom is that I have been so absorbed in trying to make this chapter interesting that now it is boring me, so I think that I will end it right here.

Dominoes

I am not really into astrology, but apparently the sign under which I am born is supposed to denote someone that likes to be the center of attention. I guess, if this were true, this would explain a lot about me. The center of attention is really just a spot for one. There really isn't room for more than that.

If this book proves anything, it might prove that I am more of an individual task person than a group player. For instance, we have the football chapter and other chapters that allude to sports and how I like to compete by myself against other people. I think that stems from the fact that I don't want to be able to get mad at or blame anyone else for mistakes and vice versa. Teammates are quick to yell at you when you have done something wrong, and slow to compliment when you have succeeded, if they are looking for their own glory. I am not saying that every athlete is like this, but most of the ones with whom I have come in contact seem to demonstrate that train of thought when they are in action. Thus, I think that all team sports and activities are just foreign things to me. All of the hoopla, the yelling, the team shirts. These things are just not for some people.

So tapping into all of my cultural influences, you can't really know that much about Southern California or the Latin Caribbean without knowing how to play dominoes. Point blank. Once, when I lived in Los Angeles, I went to a barbeque and I said that I did not know how to play dominoes. I am almost certain that the music stopped on its own. Everyone looked at me as if I had just dropped my pants and peed on the potato chips. Then ensued an emergency lesson in how to play the beloved game. I seem to remember sirens and an IV of malt liquor.

I have to admit that I didn't really learn that much,

and it really shows now.

Here on the East Coast, among my friends that I call the guys, a similar situation occurred. I confessed my dominoes virginity, and the professors of the sport got to work, trying to teach me the ins and outs of the game. So there's these little pieces of some material, and the goal is to match up numbers and outwit the other players.

It's kind of like bingo with partners and trash talking.

No matter who has tried to teach me this game, though, one thing remains certain — I am never going to learn how to play it. Everyone swears that they are going to teach me, but they try to teach me by having me play the game with them. Listen, if you are going to teach me how to drive a tractor-trailer, are you going to put me in the driver's seat in the middle of a highway and tell me to give it a go?

And even if the rest of the world can learn like that, I don't. I have to know what I am doing and why before I do it. Dominoes is something that I would have to practice. Why?

Because until I learn it, there is nothing worse than the look of a disappointed teammate looking across the table at you because you held the wrong piece too long. What's worse is that everyone else that plays the game (besides me and the dimwits that don't know how to play the game, but watch it alongside me to try to figure it out) seems to know after the first hand what everyone else has. Doesn't that take the fun out of it? More so, doesn't it take the purpose out of the game? Would you go to a fortune teller if you could read your own palm and tell your own future? So why play against someone that can basically tell exactly which pieces you have and when you are going to use them?

And then there is the whole team thing.

You have to try to figure out what your teammate has and needs by watching what he/she throws out and what turns they skip. This requires more concentration than most international spies use for reconnaissance. Is it really that serious? The last time that I tried to play, I felt like I had burst brain cells just trying to get through the third hand. I tried. I really tried, but there is no way that I am going to figure out what my teammate has and then what the two opposing players of the other team have, and manage all of those thoughts. It's like having four trains running on the same track, with no brakes. I already do that with my ADD train of thought.

Yet again, I say, this whole team thing is not for me. I want to be able to win or lose based on what I do. And that look when you are responsible for the loss — it could kill a man. You sit there with your whole dignity resting on the use of a couple of rectangular pieces of something. That's too much pressure for one person to handle.

Nope. That's all for me. It's a wonderful game for people who know it, but I think that I will stick to tennis.

Moving

Why is moving so traumatic for me? The parts of it that are troubling for most people are nothing for me. I own a bed and the rest of the things that I own are clothes and papers. The great thing about those things is that you can arrange them however you want to fit in a car or a truck or taxi or whatever. I remember someone saying something once about not getting into anything that you couldn't get out of in 15 seconds. Well, it would take me a lot longer than 15 seconds to move all of my stuff, but it is 15 seconds proportionally to the time that it takes most people to move. I guess since I did some things backwards in college, in that I lived on my own before I lived in the dorm, I have already had furniture and this and that, and I have had my fill. The next place in which I have furniture is the place that I will call home. Why do I want to get a daybed so that people can spill their drinks on it at parties, and sit on it when they come to visit, when I really want to be sitting there? Besides, when you live with other people, and you have communal furniture, you don't know what happens on those couches when you are not home.

I have considered the possibility of dousing everything that I own in gasoline and having someone with a flamethrower ignite each thing as I throw it out the window. That would be so liberating. I could sell tickets. In fact, I probably would have done it were it not for the fact that I don't have enough money to get the gas anyway.

I also have another issue now in that I have no

way to move things from one place to another. I have considered strapping the bed to my back and walking early in the morning to avoid a lot of notice and the laughs of passersby. I also have thought that I could take taxi rides back and forth, bringing this or that. I don't think that a bunk bed futon will fit nicely in the trunk of a yellow cab. Then I thought of getting someone else to walk with me from one house to another. That would require both of us getting up early to avoid stares, and then I would have to do something nice for that person for making such an extreme effort. The truth is that I am too cheap to do this, I haven't the money to be able to do this, and I don't know anyone that nice and gullible to do this for me.

The issue of moving also brings to mind the issue of the people that you live with. Roommate issues can be more stressful than raising quintuplets, more tense than Middle Eastern – U.S. relations, and more volatile than two girls at the prom with the same dress on, competing for prom queen. Being a roommate, apartment-mate or housemate is like marrying someone.

That's why having to leave the relationship is like divorce. You share intimate space with this person. This person who you may never ever so much as touch knows what your bed looks like, how you look in the morning, and how late you came in last night. So they know if you are lying when you call in sick to work the next morning with today's emergency illness. *"Hello, I have a headache in my tooth."*.

Grape Soda

I lived with three great guys one year. Of course, every group of great roommates will have a couple of flaws. This flaw was my soda. I don't know who it was (it might have even been someone from downstairs that came to visit, who knows) but someone went to town on my soda. What that colloquialism intimates is that I bought the soda, opened it, took one cup, and it was almost gone within hours. This only happened a few times, but it was preceded by the disappearance of my banana and a couple of other random fruits that I brought into the apartment. I let the first soda incident slide. I just figured that maybe someone was just really thirsty. The second incident was more egregious. Literally, I had a small cup of the soda when I left in the afternoon, grape soda, mind you, and I returned home to find the bottle in the garbage. I didn't even have the pleasure of putting my own soda into the garbage.

So, I called an Apartment meeting.

Yes, I CALLED AN APARTMENT MEETING.

Yes, I am dramatic.

No, no one else would have done that.

I am not everyone else.

A school official told me the other day that I am a "very unusual person". This is quite an understatement.

You see, every man has a favorite drink, soda,

beverage. Any man of color is particular about his food and drink, as to who is handling it, who can have some and with whom he will share it. Personally I think that there is something so strong about grape soda that would make a man kill over it. Yes, decimating his soda beyond recognition officially releases this man onto a warpath. It is an excusable sin to hurt people while in this condition. All actions executed in this state of mind are permissible by law.

So I had my meeting. I stated fervently that I had traveled to the store by bus and by foot to buy this soda, and I did not take kindly to having had only one cup of my two liter soda. I had no problem with sharing, as I was raised to share, but this went way beyond the "mi casa, tu casa" theory. This was more like "mi casa y tu casa son mis casas y no son tus casas" theory. (YAY bilingualism.! Vive bilingüismo!)

By the blank expressions after my tirade, I felt equally as relieved and full of catharsis as I felt ridiculously melodramatic.

No one ever said that I was easy to live with.

Those guys stood by me through one of the toughest times in my life and I will never forget them, especially mi medio hermano for that.

Just can't leave my grape soda there…

The Couple

I lived with the couple.

When you are in a relationship, one of the last things that you want is to become defined by your partner in apposition. An example is this: Jill, *Marvin's girlfriend,* as if Jill does not have an identity without her boyfriend. It might be worse, or really cute, depending on your take on life, when your general base of associates fuse you and your partner together because you have one identity. Being becoming to your partner is much different than becoming your partner.

Commentary aside, I lived with the couple.

Six of us lived together one year, sharing three double bedrooms. One of the rooms was occupied by two of my friends that were in a relationship together before we all moved in together. People warned us about this but we said that everything would be fine. I was part of the couple's getting together, so I especially did not foresee any problems, although then it had never occurred to any of us that the problems would be between them and us. Everyone was warning the rest of us about living with them in the case that they broke up. To this day, I wish them the best in their lives and I never stopped caring about them as people; we just can't live together.

There are many stories to relate about the couple, but this is probably the most poignant. It revolves around what is always the most important thing to me, the minute things that no one else notices but me, the things that really have no relevance on the grand scheme of things.

Remember how I am about grape soda?

I am more maniacal about my water.

I am not picky about water when I am too poor to be able to do so, but I do love my Evian when my wallet is not on a diet. One day, when my wallet was fasting, I had some lowly store brand bottled water. Nonetheless, at 3 AM, water is water. Except for in this one case.

I must preface this by stating that I am phobic of germs. (If you have any questions, please see the hygiene chapter.) So I open the fridge, thirsty as a man in the desert, and there is my water bottle with NO CAP ON IT. I start yelling as only a man of part Italian blood would do at 3 AM, gesturing in the air for no one to see. "Who took the *^&($)# cap off of my *^&($)# water jug?"

One of the members of the couple (I say it like it is a team or something) comes out of their room and asks me what's wrong. Holding my tongue, almost biting it off, I said, "Nothing, oh, nothing!"

I poured out the water. How long it had been without a cap in the fridge, I was unaware. I did notice that there was a milk container in the fridge with the wrong cap on it. You know how water and milk jugs have tops caps that match their labels? Well, my water jug's label and cap was blue, and the milk jug's label was green, yet it had a blue cap on it. Hmm… So this milk jug had what appeared to be my cap on it, and my water jug had nothing but an aperture for refrigerator condensation, odors and anything else that might have wanted to fall into the water. Thus, I rendered it undrinkable.

The next day, another member of the couple comes to my door and asks, "Was that your water bottle in the fridge?" I wanted to say, "It wasn't yours," but I managed to state, "It was before I threw it out".

Their response was, "Oh, because we lost the cap to our milk jug and we didn't know what to do. So we took the top off of the water jug and put it on our jug because we didn't want the milk to go bad. Is that ok?"

I let this go, although I did go to the computer lab and make a sign that said, "Where's the top to my water jug, #$%^&^ ?" However, later I decided to take the high road and write about it in my book instead.

My questions, however, still linger.

- Is that ok? That would have been a good question to ask yesterday, but who cares today, since I have no more water, thanks to you.
- Would the milk have gone bad in the refrigerator?
- Where could the cap to the milk jug have gone? It's not like it owns a convertible and could have escaped somewhere.
- Could we have just gotten some aluminum foil to cover it, or maybe another container in which to transfer the milk and have left my water jug

alone?

- Was that supposed to be ok?

Do you see now how having roommates is like a marriage? And then you can see how the breakup of the relationship of roommates can be like a divorce.

Imagine the five page document of grievances.

Imagine the intervention by the landlord.

Imagine the friends not speaking.

Too dramatic? Here's a flashback for you: oily floor, bloody tampon, strangers swinging in the living room (the more tawdry version of swinging, no vines here), water jug, skeevy relative with key to apartment. I say that I feel like I need alimony from that divorce. And supposedly I am the one that orchestrated the whole drama, that I am the one that threw them out of the apartment.

Of course, like I said, I wish them the best.

Life is better with water jugs safely placed in fridges with their own tops.

I lived with someone else that hid their hand soap and dishwashing liquid basically the day after I moved in.

Again, I have some questions.

- Was I going to sell the hand soap on the black market?
- Is there a large demand for stolen half-used

hand soap?

- Did it ever occur to him that I never used anything but paper disposable plates and cups?

That's ok. I mooned him. Childish, but incredibly true, and still very funny.

Being a nomad as I am, I should be used to this craziness but inevitable, I too bleed. Why is moving so hard? The unintentional ADD flow of this book is exemplified by the fact that the first two sentences of this chapter see their continuation — right now.

This is why moving is so hard. It is the last day, when the hidden hand soap, the spent grape soda, and the topless water jug fade from view and what stands foremost in your mind are the good times. The great parties and laughs from Huntington (one of my off campus apartments) and Silvers (a dorm off campus), watching Sex and the City with a cool roommate, friends of friends that become good friends from hanging out at your place, and how five or six empty rooms used to house so much life. That's what makes it hard to move.

I still don't know how I am moving my bed.

Part III

People Behaving Badly

Danger and Death

Some weird guy stalked me for a year when I was a child. He surfaced and called me to tell me how he was going to take me away to an island, where we could spend time alone and take pictures together. He told me about how he had watched me in the library when I was with my friend. I had written my name on my friend's homework by accident and he knew this as well. He knew lots about me. Then he detailed for me a list of things that I had done over the course of the past year and that is when I knew that he had been stalking me. All I knew was that he had told me over the phone that his name was Mike. The police came to question me and asked me if I knew what race the caller was. To ask that question to someone with my background is like asking a blind person which shade of green you are holding in front of them.

I was never able to figure out why he needed to take time out of his life to watch me. How could I have been that interesting at eight that a grown man would have to devote time to spying on me and being creepy? Surely there must have been something else that he could have done, like go to the bars, joined a bowling league, learned how to make a quilt or joined the Marines.

One unanswered question after another lingers in my head.

It made me very aware that I was not safe from danger or death. I drove a car with a broken steering column. I walked in the middle of a police chase albeit unbeknownst to me at the time. I gave my friend a ride one day and found out midstream that he was being pursued by armed people at that time and was armed himself. I was washing clothes when I lived in LA when an armed man ran into the Laundromat either looking for someone or was eluding someone.

I understand now that I am not safe from danger or death. I came to understand that even if I was in a padded cell with security all around me day and night, I could have an allergic reaction to the padding and die in the cell alone.

After realizing all of this, I decided that I was really not safe anywhere, so it was time to put aside my fears and take a trip somewhere. I figured that it couldn't get any worse.

Ghetto

I heard a girl, we'll call her Jen, say that her apartment was ghetto because it did not have a lot of furniture.

Really, Jen? Really?

I was listening to a top 40 radio station and a caller, let's call her Megan, calls in, commenting on a discussion about whether the DJ should wear his hat to the back or not. She says that this is so ghetto. From her voice, I made the assumption that she was not exactly the princess of the ghetto. I mean that she was not calling from the third floor apartment in the projects, if you know what I mean. Now, the way she says "ghetto" is the same tone that her mother would probably use when saying "urban," "trashy," "trailer trash," or " this milk is spoiled," with her nose turned up, as she clutches her pearls. It occurred to me that she meant ghetto as in "slumming" or "being rebellious".

However, the way that she said it was disturbing in a twofold sense — for the aforementioned reason and a second one.

As a person of color, there is an unwritten rule: I can say anything about my family, but you can't. Not even about my most pathetic, annoying relative. The same applies here. Similarly, people of color in general have been exposed to distressing socioeconomic situations in this country and, thus, have had to know the ghetto. Meanwhile, in recent times, Megans across the country have come to idolize 50 Cent as the newest teen icon and Jay-Z gets played, in the most edited form, on Top 40 radio. From these rappers and icons talking about the ghetto and their experiences, Megans now believe that they understand the ghetto. So, since these guys wear their hats backwards, Megan believes that that is so ghetto, since she now is a bona fide expert on ghetto-ness.

Little does she realize that most fashions today originated from the ghetto. Before Paris Hilton got extensions, Lakisha and Ronisha were rocking them like they were going out of style. This whole messy hair trend is what people with straight hair do to try to emulate an afro. And don't let us forget about the trend of wearing ponchos, or eating chips and salsa. El barrio, the ghetto, and other places where you have to "make do" with what you have, create trends that eventually cost too much for the people who started them to afford their high priced counterparts.

The problem is that people then making the following three associations:

> 1. That all people of color are ghetto. (Just look at Traci Bingham and that proves me correct).

> 2. That ghetto is a term that only applies to just Blacks and Latinos. (Tanya Harding and most guests of Jerry Springer that are not Black or Latino are proof of this).

> 3. That everything connected to the ghetto is bad. (Fried Chicken, basketball, and double dutch (which is now a national sport).

Thus, I guess my reaction to Megan was because I felt that she would need to really have some inkling of understanding in her life as to what is the ghetto experience before she could comment on it.

What does the word ghetto mean to you?

To some people, it means a neighborhood, like, a ghetto, what the word originally meant. It comes from an Italian dialectical word *ghèto* which meant a foundry, or a place where a foundation is built. It referred to an island where the Jews were forced to live isolated. The word comes from the word ghètar which means to cast out, which comes from the word jactare in Latin that means to throw. Yes, it was important for me to write all of that.

So, to others, it refers to where they live. It refers to a place that is not so rich, not so well kept, maybe projects or "low income housing." We're thinking of the hood, the block, an area with many of what is commonly referred to as "the corner." That is important to remember because as the suburban sprawl has reared its ugly little head, so has the elimination of corners. Have you noticed that the richer that an area is, the less corners that it has? These areas have more soft, curvy, continuous sidewalks, giving the impression of a completely harmonious and connected society.

Ghetto mentality would equate "soft corners" with being a punk. Honestly, put the suburban street against the ghetto corner and I think we all know who's winning the fight. Corners tend to be gathering places, especially in what some people call the ghetto. I think that is because this is the best vantage place to see everything, and if you are living in the ghetto, you are probably outside because you are trying to see what's going on. Thus, the corner is the best seat in the house. I hope that I don't sound too distant from the topic, although I doubt that the Ghetto Residential Association is going to come down on me too hard if I did. The point is that while it almost hurts me to see people live in such economic strain, it also hurts me to see people characterize whole races of people as what they consider to be the ghetto.

I lived close enough to the ghetto to know where it was, and not to go there. Although the word is bourgeois, the pronunciation "boo-zhee" refers to people like how I am sometimes, people of color that are viewed as viewing themselves too high or too cultured for the ghetto. I personally don't think that I think of myself as either, but just that it is not my element. For example, I remember that people would mention to me in elementary and high school when our city first got recycling bins for each house that their ghetto areas did not receive any bins, but my area, which was not ghetto, did. This is when I first noticed the disparity.

And then in more conversations, I realized that our lives were so different. These kids related to the things that they saw in "Boyz in the Hood" and movies like that. I did not even see the movie until maybe two years ago, and when I did, I did not relate to it. Some of their stories of tough love from their parents, and economic depression made my complaints about anything seem all but ridiculous. These kids had seen people sell drugs, take drugs, get shot, shoot people, and show wild reckless abandon. The most that I had ever seen was what I saw on TV. The wildest thing that had ever happened to me was that I cut school. As I did not relate, this pushed me further and further away from them, to the point that, yes, I became what they pronounce as "boo-zhee."

Be that as it may, whenever you even remotely know someone from the ghetto, you will learn a little about the ghetto attitude. Being ghetto. To me, it is not what a lot of people think. I have noticed that the word ghetto has now come to be the PC way for saying that something is "like black people, like street people, lower-class." I've heard certain people say things like that they were living ghetto, because they were living on a little bit of money, or in a ragged apartment, etc. I think that it is one of those terms that you have to be familiar with to use.

I would never describe my great day as "gnarly," not because I don't have days that fit in with the meaning of that word, but the lifestyle associated with people that use the word "gnarly" as slang is not mine. In case you were wondering, "gnarly" actually has a standard meaning, which means twisted into a state of deformity. Gnarl is a verb. Don't say you never learned anything from my book.

Now the ghetto attitude is definitely very contagious. I am going to sound like a stuffed shirt trying to explain hip-hop to the country club right now, but here goes:

The ghetto attitude is a no-holds-barred[1] "I will break you into small pieces and then come back with my whole family and beat up your whole family, grandma against grandma" type of mantra. It is caused by being in situations, both economic and social, that back one up against a wall, which forces one to fight like fire and learn how to take care of oneself. Having been pushed to that limit, or living on that limit all the time though, makes one on the defensive all of the time. A simple look turns into a challenge. Any statement not blatantly positive becomes a possible slight. It creates a very edgy,

---

[1] *(Is "no holds barred" a wrestling term? Like no type of hold is barred, which means that it's kind of free for all? Did I just figure that out all by myself? Hmmm...)

tense situation.

What happens though also is that this resistance of outside influences often means that advances toward higher education or better socioeconomic station, or at least proper diction and decorum, are also viewed as demonstrations of direct opposition to ghetto-ness and those who live in it. This sometimes means that people who speak well or are more educated are shunned and viewed as outsiders and inferior in terms of street credibility (make sure to sign me up for that degree) and also, acting as if one has ever gone to any form of school is often viewed as subordination from the code of ghetto ethics.

I have three examples of ghetto behavior that I will now share with you.

My father went to one of his doctors and upon leaving the office, requested a referral form from the ghetto girl at the desk. She insisted three times to my father that he has already received a referral, to which my father replied each time that no, he hadn't and that the doctor had just sent to get one from the desk. On the last time that my father asked, ghetto girl says, "You already got one." It could have been the bad English, or the ghetto attitude that the girl displayed, but this upset my father so much that he left. My mother returned to ask again for the referral, and this time, ghetto girl became irate. The doctor was standing by and tried to ascertain the problem. The girl showed him that, yes, she had given my father a referral. The problem was that what she called a referral was actually a receipt. The doctor asks ghetto girl if she made a habit of filing the papers that the doctor prepared for patients. She said yes. As the doctor is looking through the files, he asks if she files in alphabetical order. She says, "What you mean, LMNOP?"

I rest my case. But wait, there's more.

I mentioned in the "Chicken and Jeans" Chapter that I had someone throw a pair of jeans at me. This was my experience with ghetto shopper at Christmastime. Apparently, ghetto shopper was not too observant that I was using the folding table to fold the pile of clothes that was taller than I. How anyone could miss it, I am not sure, but she decided that she needed to toss a pair of jeans onto the table as I am folding, despite the fact that I was in the middle of folding clothes. Her utter disregard for my oh-so important work of folding (if I have to pretend like folding clothes is important to me, so much so that I am getting paid to do so, then everyone else better play along) metamorphosed into rage when she hurled the jeans at me, and in the process the sensor tag on the jeans hit me in the wrist. (Maybe she didn't hurl them in hindsight, but at the time, it seemed like she was pitching a baseball at me.)

After this, since she threw the jeans onto the folding table, I folded them, so as not to lose my rhythm and also to keep from throwing those jeans at her, or better yet, removing the sensor tag from the jeans and inserting it into her skull. She then increased the level of her audacity and said to me, "Excuse me (pronounce like "uh-scooz me"), I still want those".

So, in good corporate retail customer service fashion, I regrouped (can one person regroup?) and let her know that for future reference, that this table was where one can deposit their unwanted items from their fitting room experience. She let me know that for future reference that I was rude, and proceeded to try to tell me off, not really aware that she still needed a fitting room and had to stand there in front of me until I let her into a room. Yes, I did want to take my time deliberately to get her into a room, but really, the Christmas overflow did that job for me. Then she called me a jackass. A customer that had witnessed this whole event walked up to me as if I were in a domestic violence commercial and said to me, " You don't have to take that type of treatment. I am going to let your manager know what just happened to you." I wanted to ask her to ask them to raise my salary, but I figured that this might be too ambitious.

Anyway, my manager had a bit of a ghetto attitude herself. She literally came back to the fitting room like she wanted to fight. (She really did come back there to me taking her headset off in a way that I have only seen ghetto girls take their earring off just before a fight). She was a great manager and really cared a lot about the other employees and me. So, she came back and asked me where this customer was. She knocked on the door, and after that, though they might have been different races, ghetto-ness is what came out of both of them.

When ghetto girl said %^&* you, %^&*^ to my manager, that is when my manager lost it and went after her through the store. I have never been so happy to see a manager before, nor such an engaging cross-cultural feud. Over the headset about three minutes later, I heard my manager say, "That customer will not be returning to this store ever again".

Of course, you can't leave out the gentlemen in this arena. That was a facetious remark if you didn't pick up the humor right there. It's almost a prerequisite that as men, ghetto guys have to put each other down so as to appear greater as you stand on the backs of the downtrodden. So, I am passing by a shop where friends of a certain relative of mine worked. One of them recognized me and started talking to me about how I was doing with school. The other guy with this friend, let's call him "Stupid" for now, is a friend of my relative, and this relative has been always pretty disparaging of me, while never having amounted to anything. (Isn't that always the truth — It's the person that gained 200 pounds that wants to make fun of you because you are a little heavy, like they are the spokesperson for Weight Watchers.) So, Stupid says to me when I say that I have finished my work for my degree, "Oh, so you will be waiting on tables soon?"

Now, Stupid is meeting me for the first time and I don't want to cause a scene, but does he really know me like that to even come out of his face and say something like that? Of course, to try futilely to clean up his comment, he adds that he knows a couple of graduates that are still working at restaurants and such. I had to let him know that even if I were working at a restaurant, I would definitely be making more money than he was or could.

Then the subject came up about my major. Stupid mentions that it was ridiculous for me to be an

Therapy for No One in Particular

English major since I grew up speaking English. Besides the obvious example of his lack of English ability to demonstrate that growing up in an English speaking country does not speak to your ability to speak or write the language, I had to help him to understand that, no, Stupid, I did not study verbs and adjectives, that this major deals with literature. Then I had to break it down for him that, yet again, with my experience, degree, and ability, I would definitely be able to get a job doing something much more productive than his present occupation of standing on the street corner. (I don't know that to be a fact, but I felt better being under that impression.) And still, he appeared unfazed and relentless in his ghetto self-righteousness, looking down upon me because I don't feel the need to sell drugs, have various children out of wedlock with odd names and crazy mothers, or scratch my genitals and hold onto them for dear life at every waking moment.

On the way to finish this chapter, I was almost accosted by an 8-year-old boy who gave me the meanest scowl that I have seen on this side of the world. (The ghetto term for this is that he gave me an "ice grill".) He was on a little bike, appropriate for his age, and drove up next to me and, while still pedaling, slowed down and stared me down like I had stolen his ice cream. He then peddled away, about 30 feet more, and then, for no apparent reason, stopped, threw the bike down and sat down on the ground with a look on his face that said, I have had it, and I am not taking anymore from you, this bike, or this day. The only thing that I could think of that could have fueled his anger was that I had just been in the bodega (corner store) and I bought a strawberry soda (which you can only purchase in the ghetto, of course) and maybe I bought the last one.

Or not.

That's just how the ghetto is. Peace out homies. It's official like a referee with a whistle.

Treatise: Apology to All

I always wanted to write something that had "treatise" in the title.

An autobiography makes note of all that a person has accomplished. A true account of a life, though, I think, should include an accounting for transgressions. I attempt to do that here.

I apologize to the universe and its maker for mistakes that I have made in search of my own selfish desires, the desires of the flesh.

I am sorry for all the misuse of others' emotions and time in search of a simple embrace or affection.

I apologize to the person who first stole my heart for not telling her soon enough, but in a way, I thank her for opening the door to love freely.

I apologize to God for unintentionally ignoring Divine guidance and misusing the gifts that I have been given.

I apologize to myself for failing to try things that I should have tried before, for not believing in myself and for loving myself too much at times, and for not releasing this book sooner.

Ok, now back to our regularly scheduled program.

Talk Show

I am making a concerted effort this week to see my friends, live a little dangerously, spend money happily and wisely, and not answer too many questions. People ask too many freaking questions. I think that living in a culture of talk shows and fictional police dramas has made us all a little too inquisitive for no good reason. You can't just say hi anymore to anyone without feeling like you have been sequestered by Barbara Walters. It is like a disease.

I went to visit this girl, and for the first like 10 to 20 minutes, she asked me questions, and I answered them. The next day, I was online, and all that this other girl continued to do was ask me question, after question, until I had no more answers. It seems that people can't just have conversations anymore. They have to steer what is happening with their questions, so that they can have control, in truth, like it is their own talk show. I have never really had that much to ask someone. I understand that we ask questions to find out what we want to know, but what amount of information does acquaintance entitle us? This girl asked me if I was still sad about my father's death. Someone asked me to explain in detail how it feels to have a loved one die. Someone turned to me on a bus once and asked me, "What are you?" The world has gone crazy with curiosity, and if the saying holds true, then we will have a lot of dead cats in this world.

So the more and more that I think about it, I realize that this trait is becoming extremely pervasive in our culture. I was really not in the mood to talk one day, and all it seemed that people wanted to do was ask me questions.

Person: So what are you doing?

Me: Nothing.

Person: What did you do today?

Me: Not much.

Person: Blah Blah Blah?

Me: Some answer I gave.

Person: Blah Blah Blah?

Me: Some other answer

Person: What's wrong with you?

Me: Nothing.

Person: There's something wrong with you. You are always talking.

Me (thinking that I want to say thanks to this person for calling me a big blabbermouth): Sometimes, I just don't want to say much.

This is the part of the conversation when I want to make up something so that the person will go away, and I say something like that it has been a very long day, or that I am thinking about something, I am not feeling too well, or the like. All of these are true. The person is making my day much longer. I am thinking about how much I want to destroy this person for making my day worse with all of these blasted questions and comments. And, I am really not feeling too well — I am sick of this person.

Sometimes this is not a bad thing, but I still believe that talk shows and TV cops have trained us to question and respond like Ricki Lake and her trailer trash or ghetto-fabulous guests. A classic example, although it was actually more poignant that I make it appear, is when I was talking to my friend. We'll call her Aura (she would like the comparison). After my father passed, I would find myself talking to her, and letting down my guard, and crying, etc., all the grief related stuff. However, one day, it became obvious to both of us what was happening. Every time that I would talk to her, and she would ask me questions to elicit my feelings, and I would feel the need to keep purging my soul. This kept happening until one day we both realized that each time we talked, she had the same nature sounds music playing. For some reason, this put us in the talk show mode, the talk show episodes where there is the serious soft music, over which they usually say something like, "Mary, here's your father", or "You are a survivor" and Kleenex is being used like it is going out of style in five minutes.

This is exactly what I mean. We have been trained by all of these freaking shows when and how we are supposed to talk, and ask and answer questions, including how to react to certain music.

So, today, I have no comment to anyone's questions.

The Computer Lab at School

The little bald headed man is going to drive me insane.

Every time that I come to the computer lab at school, which has to be about every day of my life, I feel like I run into the same people. I do spend a lot of time here, so that is inevitable.

The important part of this is that I have noticed over the course of my association with this school that the computer lab workers have turned into this society or subculture. As with many job settings, they seem to fraternize well, which is not abnormal.

Mostly everything is normal except for two outstanding features, overzealous people and the little bald headed guy.

Overzealous people, let's call them op's, do this. They buzz around the lab like they have wings, not even allowing someone to be able to go to the bathroom, without logging them off, moving their stuff and cleaning up the area for someone else. I have witnessed enough to know that I am not the only one that has seen this happen. They make sure that no one, I mean, not even God himself gets any more than two copies of their printout. I know that is their job, but the urgency connected with this effort is displayed with more diligence than an FBI operative.

That is not as bad as the closing time situation, however.

The lab closes at 8:30 Monday to Thursday, at 6:30 on Friday and 7 on Saturday and Sunday during this summer. These things never change.

And granted, there are a lot of people that do not use the lab as frequently as I, so they might not be aware of all of the ins and outs of the lab, including its hours.

All of that aside, there is this guy that works there, a little bald headed guy, to whom I was quite cordial until one day, he showed me his overzealous side. On this day, he literally logs my friend off of his computer maybe five minutes after my friend and I had just logged in. This might have been because my friend left for a moment to say hi to someone, but that other person was almost within arms reach of where our computers were. It was so obvious that this was a lesson in micromanagement.

So when I asked him what he was doing, he reacted as if I were the strange one, or as if I were talking out of turn in a second grade classroom. God forbid that someone should step away from their computer for a moment and not sit attentively and reverently into the divine space of pixels in front of them. Anyway, as I showed him that my friend was literally two paces behind him, he muttered something, probably cursing me out in binary code, and walked away. This is when I started to notice his closing time shtick.

To put this in perspective, usually someone from the lab announces at intervals of an hour before, a half hour before, 20 minutes before, 15 minutes before, 10 minutes and 5 minutes before closing. He however seems to have found this duty to his one small soapbox in life, the one minute stage in which he can expunge the bile of his soul unto the masses of typists and last minute paper writers. It's always in this unnecessarily condescending tone. Instead of the regular announcement that everyone else says (It's ____. The lab will be closing in ____ minutes. Please wrap up your work, blah blah blah...), he feels the need to add in some extra comment.

Sometimes, it's 'if you haven't yet made your way to the printer, please do so at this time'. Sometimes it is "The building will close at ____. Please prepare to leave by then'. It's a bit hard to express the bitter sarcasm of his words. It is probably better to imagine what it is like to be the conductor for the last train leaving NY on Saturday nights. It seems like you should be able to say anything since the drunk people on the train are amused by anything, and the sober people are too drained to respond to your nonsense. This is about the size of it.

And this is where most of this book has been concocted. Trying to get out before closing time at the computer lab.

I have had to say, I have met a lot of great people here that have been really helpful, really nice. There is one guy who works there with his brother. They always say hi to me, and we joke around like old buddies. People like them make it ok to deal with the bitter bite of some of the other people that work there. I guess it's like what happens with any job.

I felt compelled to write about this because as I was reflecting on my life here at this school, there are very few days that pass by in which I don't visit the lab to do my work. I feel like I work there sometimes. It is a canvas for my writing space, and like it or not, in a weird way, it's a necessary little part of my existence. There are emails that I have written there, songs that I have concocted there, poetry that I have recorded there, requests for assistance or replies to such requests that I have dispensed there, and all of these are part of the fabric of the patchwork that is my existence as a student. The fact that I was able to conjure so much sentiment in the last paragraph indicates to me that I really need to buy a computer of my own.

Nothing

This is another day that I am busy doing nothing. I was supposed to go the gym, to write a chapter, to be really productive. I was really on a roll. It started with an interview in the morning and somehow, in between then and now, I decided, no — I don't want to do anything. I want to grab a bag of chips and salsa and sit down somewhere and do absolutely nothing.

I think that is a good idea

Hygiene – My Way

There is nothing in your nose that needs to go into your mouth. That is one of the worst things that I can ever see a person do. Why would you think that it makes any sense that something that is impeding you from breathing fully, that resembles an alien life form, should be taken from your nose and put into your mouth?

It is bad enough that so many people pick their noses. Really. I understand that sometimes the mucus is lodged into your nose in such a way that just blowing your nose will not move it. That is perfectly understandable. All of us have had to dig in our nose, and the person that denies it is not human. However, the buck stops there, pal. Get a tissue, clean your hands and keep it moving. That's all. The mucus goes in the garbage, you go on your way, and we are all happy campers. What makes a very hostile, irate camper is first when people don't clean their hands after digging in their nose. Here I must make a very important distinction. Scratching the bridge of your nose with the back of your hand or the side of your finger, that is not unsanitary. What I mean is to touch the outside of your nose does not make your finger dirty. Essentially, it does, as dirty as touching other parts of your skin, but what I mean is that it is definitely not the same situation as digging into your nose.

Ok, back to the matter at hand.

Yes, going for the nasal gold is really a private issue, between you, a secluded location, and your tissue. No one needs to know about that. I will never shake hands with someone who I have seen dig in their nose, and I will wash my hands after every time I shake hands with someone that I think has done that. The reason for the latter is that some people are slicker than others with this "picking of the nose in public" issue. Some people do it in such a way where it is almost not noticeable, except if you have a keen sense for hygiene. Regardless, I think that those people are even worse, because at least the people that do it outrightly are not conscious that this is not only not sanitary, but is not socially acceptable. The sneaky ones know that this is quite nasty, and persist in doing it anyway, almost in an exhibitionist way.

There is a similar issue with the face. Popping pimples and the like are definitely behaviors that should not be shared with anyone. This is for the privacy of your bathroom. Get an exfoliating lotion, a loofa, a scrub, a facial, a wad of toothpaste (the college face cream), get a bathroom, and go to town. You should want people to compliment you on your complexion. No one wants to share in your process of clearing your face, no matter how liberating of an experience it may be.

Farts. I am not the average guy when it comes to this issue. Don't share your gases with me. If you don't sneeze on me, or cough on me, why fart in a room with me? That is the worst gas that the body can expel, so, if your body doesn't want it, why should mine? It is like toxic waste pollution.

People think that it's funny, cool, something that people should accept. Especially other guys. I was not raised in a barn, so I don't do things like animals. I am not sure what my biggest objection to it is — the smell or the fact that I am sharing a nasty, unsanitary experience with someone. However, the fact remains —it's not attractive, it's not funny, and worse yet, it's got to be bad for your underwear. It becomes the filter for the release of your effluvium, and I would imagine that after a while, that renders them useless. This farting culture is probably a bigger explanation for the creation of colored briefs and the popularity of boxers, which are usually not white. Yes, farting to me cannot be the best look for white undergarments.

I am going to not say much about the bathroom except this: No one wants to know what you did in the bathroom. I could care less how close we are. I would rather that you would stick your finger in my eye than that you would forget to flush the toilet, or leave anything on the seat other than the ceramic or whatever substance from which toilet seats are made. That was there before you got there. Yes, the point is that the bathroom should look just the same way it did when you came in there.

For instance, once, at a party at my house, someone decided to sit on the towel/magazine cabinet/rack. I knew this not because I saw them do it or that they told me; no, I knew this because when I saw the bathroom later on, the bent metal fixture indicated to me that someone was raised by wolves and obviously could not figure out where to sit down, not that there is any reason to sit down in a bathroom except the obvious.

Ladies, special note. I don't know what goes on with you girls and tampons, and I don't want to know. I don't want to see my blood, so I don't want to know about yours. Also, hair in the sink — definitely not attractive. That could be the end of a relationship for me. If you are in the shower, or are combing your hair in the bathroom, check the drain. It's really nasty, and worse yet, it can't be ignored. If you don't clean it out, someone has to, or eventually there will be a clog the size of a small nation. Once, one of my former roommates and his date took their bedroom matters into the shower, and I knew this because not only did she not clean the drain of her hair, but on top of that hair was, well, let's just say a special conditioner that I did not need to find out that she uses. So, please, from someone who has experienced girls that don't care or don't remember about hygiene, do it for me, for your mom, for yourself, do it for someone.

Keep it clean or I get mean.

The Correct Pronunciation of Chitterlings

I am a big mixture of cultures, and I don't really claim just one, so I see myself as a good stew of world spices. I grew up in a town with mainly people of color in my schools, so I was exposed to various cultures inside and outside of my home. Many times, especially after seeing my parents, my friends had questions, both understandable and bizarre. Like these:

Are you mixed?

What is your father?

What is your mother?

Were you born in this country?

Where are you from?

Did you grow up confused?

These questions I definitely understood. Here is one that made no sense to me:

What do you eat for dinner?

I would never think to ask someone something like that. That just seems like such an inconsequential thing in terms of who I am. Then again, I guess as well that food is a cultural marker and a piece of identity.

We were all picky eaters growing up, so my mom often cooked more than one kind of vegetable, or picked up something from a restaurant for one or more of us. Some people said that she was spoiling us, but hey, if I don't eat peas, I don't eat peas. If the smell of lima beans makes me sick, placing a plate of them in front of me is not going to make me eat them any more quickly. Why waste it on me when there are starving kids in other countries that would love to eat that food? (I don't know about you, but if I was starving, and someone gave me lima beans or peas to eat, I probably would still starve. Let's be real. Hunger doesn't create delirium until after a while.)

Anyway, one day I went to the local bodega, and I noticed something the produce section called chitterlings. I asked the owner what that was and he told me that he didn't know himself and that he had ordered it for someone that had requested it. When I got home, I asked my mother the same question. She smiled and asked me if I had ever heard someone say "chit-lins". I said yes, in school. She told me that this is the way that most people pronounce chitterlings as such. Chitterlings are the intestines of hogs. It smells like crap, for the obvious reason, from what I am told, since I have never had them nor am I rushing to try them. My mother told me that in harder times, folks had to use every part of every animal to try to stretch out their dollar. This was especially true before the slaves were freed, when they really had to take what they could to survive.

I am more of an Italian and Latin food kind of guy, but I always thought this story was kind of endearing, if not for the fact that I must have asked this question three years ago.

I love being a melting pot.

The Smell and Taste of Yesterday

When I was about four, someone tried to kill me.

If you have read anything in this book, you should know now that nothing is unbelievable in my life. Here's some of the odd things that relate to my senses of smell and taste and my memory.

- I was visiting the home of a family friend and I asked for water. I did not know what it was, but whatever the person gave me had a really strong smell, something that I did not want. I think that a little bit did get in my mouth, but I stopped before I could really start drinking. About 14 years later, I was cleaning something and I was using ammonia. This was my first time using ammonia to clean something. As soon as I opened the bottle, the memory came back to me and it was clear that the person 14 years ago had handed me a good old cup of ammonia.

- Once, I took a test drive in California at a Saturn dealer. I had been really hungry, and I asked the salesman if he had any candy. The only thing that he had was a Breath Assure capsule. It uses some kind of oil to combat bad breath odors. I am not sure what the oil is, but as soon as I put the capsule in my mouth, it unlocked a memory of when I was assaulted by a school worker in second grade.

- I started to talk about this in the Hygiene chapter, when I referred to the toxic waste butt situation. I used to work with a man that was probably 400 pounds. The problem wasn't his weight; it was that almost every pound of him smelled, reeked of toxic human funk. I complained to my superiors that he was emitting toxic fumes into the air, and as I stated before, if your body doesn't want your smell, then why should I? After two days of being on vacation, I passed by a dumpster and immediately thought of work. I was feeling like I should be going the other way to the bus stop or that I had forgotten to go in to work that day. It was then that I realized that the man smelled like a dumpster. He was finally put in a room by himself, but that only contained his smell in this little room that became a virtual office stink bomb.

- Sambuca reminds me of my dad. Not that he ever really drank, but this was the one drink that I know that he liked.

- The cologne Curve also reminds me of my dad. At first, it reminded me of watermelon, and I hate watermelon, and I also wasn't too close with my dad, so I never really liked the cologne. Now that he's gone, it just reminds me of him. I have a container of it in my room.

- Pears remind me that sometimes you can't ever really have what you want, as I love the taste and smell of pears, but I am allergic to them.

Birthday

Today is my birthday. Normally, since I did not celebrate my birthday growing up, I don't do anything for my birthday. It's a bit illogical when you think about it. Your birthday is the day that you were born. Even the verb construction of that statement is passive. I didn't do anything but just be born. It's not even like I allowed myself to be born — I had no say in the matter. My mother did all the physical work in that regard. All of her children were born by Caesarean section (C-Section) and, if anything, all thanks should go to her and to God. She should get a medal of honor for that, because if I were a woman, adoption would be the only way that I would be having a child.

Anyway, so, my birthday is not an accomplishment of my own for me to celebrate. It is a day that the cycle of life begins again. A year's worth of musing and ups and downs is what this day represents. However, there is one gift that I would long for on this birthday — and that would be to have my dad again.

This is my first birthday without him and it is extremely weird. I didn't think that it would affect me so badly, but I can't do my yearly reflection that I normally do on my birthday without having so many thoughts of him coming back to my head. I have said this once or twice since he died, once while holding his ashes, but:

I miss you Dad.

Through all the good and bad times, I could always count on you to be there, no matter what. Your physical absence from this world means that my life has changed drastically.

I know that you can't change the past, but to see him lifeless while holding his hand as the respirator and all machines giving "0" for his levels, flat-lined, is still a bit much for me. However, it was even harder for him to live. I would have given my life to save his, regardless of our differences. It would have only been fair for me to give my life for the one that gave me life. Part of me doesn't see the justice of his death while I have my life. I have learned though that one thing about life is that it is often not fair.

Tomorrow is the five-month anniversary of my dad's death. I'm going to try to celebrate life this week, not my birthday.

Live while you can because you can't when you're dead. Sometimes I find true enjoyment in stating the obvious.

OK Outfits, and Almost Beautiful

Ok, so I was saying that I sounded like I was on the cast of "Mean Girls" for my comments about Ugly Boy. I do not apologize for them, but I do want to say something else that will really make me seem like I wrote that movie about my life. There are two groups of people about whom I will speak right now for whom I feel sorry. Who am I to feel sorry for someone, you may ask, but I realize that my life was sadder when I was not conscious of my misgivings and how to make the best of bad situations. So, I give you two groups that deserve a national charity.

First group is the Ok Outfit people. Such as the moms that buy the big purple coat because that is all that they can afford at Burlington Coat Factory after buying their child the most expensive outfit. Such situations like these seem to make people feel that they have to be part of the OK outfit crew. What does that mean? It is the segment of the population that seems to feel that is OK because of their finances or other reasons for them to just buy whatever color, shape and size outfit, and call it a day.

I feel really sorry for people that wear gray more than necessary. There is a classy gray and a garbage gray. I mean the garbage gray here. There is nothing wrong with the color and I even wear it at times. However, this is not a color that should clothe your body on a regular basis. There is a guy that works at my school who apparently has no other colors in his closet except for gray. I think that if I were him, that would automatically make me put myself in therapy.

This gray fetish is scary, like one's whole outlook on life is colorless, lifeless, bland. I've seen people like that all through my life and I've never ceased to be amazed by this.

The other group is Almost Beautiful. Almost Beautiful is this person: She walks into a room and people can't help but stare, stunned by her beauty. She has on the right blouse and the pants that accentuate every curve. Her hair and make-up are perfect.

And then you realize that what everyone was staring at was the fact that she had on bright pink sneakers.

Ok, so maybe this is drastic, but that is a dramatization of Almost Beautiful. Almost Beautiful is those people who basically have everything it takes to be stunning, except that one little correctable flaw that remains as of yet unchecked.

For instance, there is the screwed-up-shoes guy. He will have the whole outfit, but his whole outfit looks like the remnants from a fire or from a World War II battle. There is the bad hairstyle girl that has what it takes to be a model, but whatever is on top of her head is paying tribute to Jersey Hair.

Why do I care about these people?

I've been OK Outfit boy, when I reasoned that everything went with black, so I should just wear anything with black shirts or black ties. I've been "almost handsome," and I have had those scuffed shoes. I've even been the extreme case of "Almost handsome" wearing OK outfit. So when I see these people, I know where they are at in their lives, and I want to rescue them. I want to rush them in an ambulance to a mall and get all their style problems corrected, like emergency surgery.

Got to Get it Tight, Got to Get it Right

I was five when I was first introduced to the wonderful world of dieting. Two of my relatives sequestered me in the kitchen and showed me a salad as if it was the Holy Grail. I was told how I needed to be on a diet. I don't think that I really understood what a diet was at five.

I know now.

I know what diets are, the meaning of fats, carbohydrates, body mass indicators, pilates and yoga. I've learned so much about dieting and weight loss that I feel like I can write a book on it. (Maybe I will if I ever finish this one.)

After I broke up with my ex-fiancée, I decided to drop all of my inhibitions and enter a gym. Basically, I emerged from there 80 pounds lighter. Then I hit that plateau where I didn't lose anything or gain anything. That's more frustrating than being in a war with a gun full of ammo, trying to shoot people, but your gun is jammed.

Then my loss started happening again when I embarked on what I called, "My 90-day Plan to be a Sexier Man". It's been a lot of hard work, but I have been happy to see my results. My body is starting to take the form that I always wanted and always knew was somewhere under my skin. My newest inspiration is not a diet. Diets are for doodle heads. (That's my statement; you can quote me on that.) It's not a reunion or a wedding for which I am toning. It's just good old me. I have inspired me.

That and a little help from Beyonce and Trinity from the Matrix.

Trinity (laying on her back having jumped down a flight of stairs): "Get up!"

Beyoncé (on getting herself in shape): "Got to get it tight, Got to get it right."

What else would you expect from me but to have these aphorisms run my fitness life?

For me, though, I have always had a problem with my weight. I have always been heavy. It seems to me that skinny people have more issues with trying to be skinny or skinnier than a lot of bigger people including me have had with always been thick and wanting to see a change.

For instance, this girl I knew that I used to tutor, let's call her Lisa, used to obsess over weight issues. Of course, like I have intimated a little earlier, when you are not small, you think that everyone that is smaller than you are should have no problem with body image. I have learned differently thanks to Lisa and others that I have met that, to me, seem like waifs, but to them, seem like whales awaiting harpooning. She was a really nice girl, and I thought that she was quite attractive, to be honest.

Anyway, so I am in the middle of tutoring her, when one of her roommates comes into the kitchen area. Roommate approaches and asks everyone in the kitchen, "Did you eat my ice cream?" This impassioned plea reminded me of the best soap opera moments that only make sense in a world of complete make-believe. I have never heard someone so concerned about food, especially a dessert. (Well, there *was* that time when I flipped out because my father ate my apple cinnamon pancakes, but even the drama king that I am, I didn't react this vehemently.) It was like a mother looking for her child, or how Hello Kitty would be if she could lament why she has no mouth. (Of course, if she had a mouth, which the stuffed Hello Kitty Dolls and the drawn cartoon version don't, this would nullify her need to have this discussion. You get my drift.)

So, she went to each person in the house to ask them if they were responsible for demolishing her ice cream supply.

So when it became clear that the culprit was not present, or might have been too afraid to face her wrath at the moment, she went on to relate to us, almost tearfully how she had "bought this ice cream so that" she could "eat for a week". No, she had not bought peanut butter and jelly or a chicken, or even crackers. She bought a half gallon of ice cream for a week's worth of nourishment. However, the ridiculousness does not stop there.

So she tells us how she had no money now, not even enough to put gas in her car to go to work. (It would seem that she should have wanted to work more, if she had to be put in this situation.) She had bought this half gallon of frozen cream heaven so that she would not starve and someone decided to eat almost all of it. In her defense, the half gallon had really been decimated as if a plague or a hungry nation had devoured it.

She left a letter for the culprit and she read it to us. Basically, it read:

"Hi. I hope that you enjoyed my ice cream. That was all that I had to eat for this week. Here's the rest of it to finish since you liked it so much. I hope that you are planning to buy me another one."

It is to be noted that this note was read to us with the seriousness of a president declaring war on the world.

How surprising, then, is it to find out that one of the girls in the house was later diagnosed with bulimia? Apparently, after months of mysterious food decimation, this one girl was caught scarfing down another roommate's food, and the girls of the house put two and two together. This is proof that everyone's battle is different and offers different challenges.

Being Wack

This chapter is dedicated to wack people. What do I mean by that? There are just some people in this world that I have come across that definitely are not cool and never will be. I am not speaking about the nerds of the world, the geeks, the misfits. Some of those people in actuality are pretty cool in their own little world and their own right. I don't look down on them. I have to say, some of them might be a lot better company and better human beings than the people that I am about to describe. No, wack to me is this: People that treat other people like garbage to satisfy the endless void that they have in their baseless souls. Let's speak about some of these people, shall we...

Some of these people are friends of ours and some are enemies. They are all annoying.

They all seem somehow to be products of Misdirected Aggression. Let me give you a scenario. At college, I have run into what I call the computer lab thug. They are these guys that walk around like they just came out of a 50-Cent video, with all the latest clothes on, and the swagger. You know what I mean by the swagger. It's the "I'm the hottest thing on the streets, nobody can step to me, I get all the girls, my *&^% don't stink" walk. It's the walk that when recognized would normally make one a little nervous in a dark alley, or a little self conscious if you see a pack of guys with this walk passing you in the mall, because you know that one of them is going to make a disparaging comment about you.

The thing to remember is that the computer lab thug has adapted this walk, but...here's the clincher. He is really not a thug. He was a straight A student in high school. Ok, let's not give him that much credit — let's at least say that he was a decent student, and maybe, maybe, got in trouble once or twice. Now when he gets to college, he has a major decision to make. Does he continue in this life of mediocrity, or does he reinvent himself? Yes, folks, after a couple of days after his graduation from Main Street High School, he decides that he is going to recreate himself into American Badass Extraordinaire. He is now going to be the biggest mack of the university. He is going to have everyone in fear. He has a whole summer to concoct his stories of gang warfare, sexual prowess, and a bitter childhood, all of these things to make himself seem like the bad boy gone good. It gives him the edge that he so needed in Simpletown USA, but just never managed to achieve.

This formula can work if you move from Michigan to New Jersey, but the problem here is that most of the computer lab thugs are coming here from maybe 30 to 40 minutes away, maybe Jersey City or Union City, and along with them are other people from their town and school who really know their story.

Here's a few more examples of wack people.

College Punk

For example, there is College Punk. That is my code name for a person that I know that swears that I am the dirt off of the ground that is on the bottom of his shoe. He has been a thorn in the side of my existence since I met him. I always say that he looks at me like either wants to fight me or get my phone number or both. He still, even after having graduated two years ago, tries to perpetuate his "hardcore" image. He sends messages through people about how he doesn't like me. He actually had the gall to shake my hand this year. A real thug doesn't go back on his word. In that sense, I respect a street thug or a goon or anyone of that ilk more than I do him.

Ugly Friend

Then there are the people that have always thought that they were God's gift to the world, and have no shame about sharing this with people. This is your Ugly Friend that swears that he gets all the girls, or that all the guys are after her. (Don't act like you don't have ugly friends. Everyone has an ugly friend. Even ugly people have ugly friends. I am not overly judgmental; not everyone can be pretty...)

They act as if they were completely unaware of their flaws, both physical and in personality. They act so oblivious to this that you are almost inclined to believe, even for a moment, that this person really is God's gift to the world.

However, really soon, they remind you of the implausibility of this, when they tell you how they slept with the hottest girl on campus, or how this girl is so enamored with him, or how the hottest girl on campus used to be his girl. Ugly Friend as a girl will give you the only attitude when there is the slightest chance that someone might be talking to them more than to say "excuse me", "what's your friend's name?" or "could you pass me a napkin?"

The Leech

The Leech is the emotionally needy person that needs you always to support them or help them figure out things for them. They want to go where you go because they fear being alone with their own thoughts. They have you to come with them anywhere that they might have a chance of being uncomfortable. You are like the bumpers to their car.

The Wimp

The wimp is a great person except that they have no backbone whatsoever. Pure jellyfish infrastructure. They are great to party with, laugh with, even to talk to about your problems. When they are upset, they will go for days, weeks, years even, without even giving the slightest hint as to what is wrong. It is worth it for them to not have a confrontation than to rid themselves of what is in their heads and hearts. They actually hurt the relationship more than they could ever help it by doing this. Dealing with the wimp is more trying than trying to discern five pages worth of information from a mime.

Nosy

This is the friend/acquaintance that needs to know everything about you, everything about what you are doing and anything in the world, just to know. They need to be kept abreast of everything in your life and never out of the loop. Nosy person is like your personal paparazzi.

Supercool

Supercool is like Ugly Friend but just in terms of coolness. The person swears that they are the life of the party, or more specifically, that they invented the party, and that people await their arrival everywhere. From major events to the bathroom. Supercool has mastered the art, at least to himself/herself, of being suave and debonair. Little do they realize that none of us live in their reality.

I have friends and foes that fall into every one of these categories. I am probably one of these types of people in someone else's eyes. The beautiful thing about this book being my book is that I get creative license to never be wack in my own creation.

Sometimes Serious (Dissolve)

I am a frivolous person at times. I like to have fun. I like to joke around and have a good time.

Then there are those moments.

There are moments when I am lost so deep that it

doesn't even make any sense. There are times when tears would not even relieve the frustration that lies deep beneath my pores and within my thoughts. These are the times when a simple touch could probably stir up the deepest emotions. A word could set off a bad mood. These are the days that I think that Prozac wouldn't be such a bad idea.

And then there are the days that I reflect on my father.

I still have a problem understanding that I don't have a father in the flesh anymore. Just a couple of nights ago, I was in my mom's house and I fell asleep on my father's side of the bed. I actually didn't fall asleep until much later. For a while, I was staring into the nothingness that is the numbness of denying the loss of a loved one. I thought that the first few days would be the hardest, but that was just the beginning. No, the hard parts are lying on my father's side of the bed, looking off into space, wondering if my grandfather felt alone when he died alone in a hospital bed. Wondering if I would be going through the same cancer as my grandfather and father endured. Wondering if I have it now. Wondering why I am wandering through this life like the way his last few days were. I have felt like a zombie, or better yet, I feel like I am trapped in someone else's body, with no way to escape.

These are the days that I most want to be able to be busy and just forget what has happened. I don't want to think about them since I think about it all the time. In an hour, it will be three months. I have trouble sleeping. I have trouble sleeping because for one time in my life, my father was not troubled or bothered, and that moment will trouble me for the rest of my life.

I sometimes contemplate what he was thinking about before he went into his coma. I wonder a lot what was going on in his head the last day of his life. I know that they told us that he lost a lot of his brain from the strokes that he had the last week of his life, but I still need to believe in some way that he did not lose all capacity to ponder life and love and my family. Then again, it would probably be best to know that he was not thinking of a thing, and was just resting, and that he was in no way aware of the craziness that was happening in his body during those last 10 days.

I wonder if he was happy that we got a chance to talk the day before. When I was talking to him, he was having trouble breathing. I found out later that this was partly because he was beginning at that moment to have his heart attack.

I started this chapter and it has taken four months to return to it to complete it. I am still numb, as if someone left me in the freezer since he died. It is part of my reality that his reality is no more, and this has created somewhat of a sub-reality for me.

Sometimes, it's not that I want to die, but I just don't have the patience to wait to see if I will get through another day. I find myself recently lacking the willpower to make all the decisions and do all of the actions that are required to continue. These are my serious days.

These are the days that I walk down the street and stop walking, hoping, praying, that I could just dissolve into the ground and slip into nothingness. These are the days that I feel purposeless and the opposite of driven.

I wonder on these days if I will always be alone. Will I always be depressed and empty?

These are the days that I look for, and dread, the days that have accompanied me since I was a child, like an obedient puppy, never biting me, but never leaving my side. This is when I loathe my body and mind, libido and conscience. This is when it all matters and simultaneously nothing is important enough to capture my attention.

This is the depression that opposes the mania, since I think that all humans on the continuum of sanity are just different levels of bipolar.

My sixth grade teacher died this year as well. She died at the beach, while sun tanning. Avoiding my quips about the ridiculous nature of this accident, I turn to ponder this situation. I wonder what she was thinking in her last moments. Was it ridiculously glorious to die in the blaze of the sun? I hope that her last thoughts were peaceful.

I hope that mine are as well.

Fingerpaint

It takes dedication to write a book. I have learned the truth of this. I feel like every author that I have ever seen portrayed in every movie that I can remember. There are those days when you have the proverbial writer's block, when nothing seems worthy of your attention to write it, let alone someone to read it. There are the deadlines that you have to meet and more.

The reason that I mentioned all of these things is because when you are just an unknown writer, there is always the added pressure that only you really believe that you are a writer.

It seems easier for people that you know believe that you are going to be a millionaire from selling beach front property in Texas than to believe that you are an author who will publish.

When you tell people that you are working on a book, it becomes this nice thing that they say "aww" about. At first, it is nice, but then it becomes really annoying that you are letting people know about this work that means a lot to you, this work of blood and sweat and tears, and they react as if you are in kindergarten, showing them your fingerpaint portrait. Save the "awws" for your little rugrat.

I have this one friend that never seemed to understand when I said that I was busy writing my book. This friend would always then persist to ask me what I was doing, ask me when I was going to be done, as I am writing. It's not a like a memo or a term paper. This is a book, first of all. Secondly, it is a book about my life. I am still living my life. Some days, I have been walking down the street and it occurs to me that I have completely forgotten to cover some very important and specific area of my life and this would render me negligent if I did not include this in the story of my life. Some days, I know exactly what I need to add to a chapter. The point is, my time is dictated by the ever changing needs of the book. I can't tell my book, oh, let me take this creative time away for you because my friend is bored and does not want to be in the house alone. I realize that I have to make time for everything and be balanced; however, creativity does not really have a time schedule. Inspiration does not punch in and out of the office every day. These things happen when they happen and you really have to run with it.

This is not something that a lot of people understand.

People understand work. People understand schedules. People don't understand the mania of being your own boss, when your project is creating your own end result, especially when that end result is an encapsulation of your own life. It is a pretty insular experience. Most other professions outside of the art world cannot relate. A truck driver might be his own boss, but it's not like he is going to be driving on his road and paving it at the same time. A hairdresser might manage herself in her shop, but her services basically all relate to end results for other people.

Add to this that some people think that this is incredibly easy or fun. It is interesting to reflect on your life in that way that I have through writing this book a specific way. It does intrigue me to learn so much about myself and see that process crystallize into something brilliant, at least to me. However, like I mentioned in another chapter, it is an addictive and arduous process. It is addictive in that I am so interested in seeing where the project takes me that I am ready to sacrifice so much time to see it happen. It is arduous because it is so much work to try to give the fullest picture of me while still conveying my thoughts and beliefs in a pleasing manner.

I think it would be either so much easier or so much harder to try this when I am like 75.

Anyway, regardless of what people think or expect, I am proud that I have embarked upon this process of artistic expression and self-discovery. It is fun, informative and life-changing.

It has also makes me realize how much I have done and how far I have left to go.

It also makes the concept of "chapters" of one's life really, really cliché.

Part IV

Just Some Guy's Survival Guide

Free Flan
(in an Aluminum Circular Thing)

I have never been so nervous buttering a roll.

One thing that you learn as a student is that you go where free food is served. Being a student means being broke. Broke becomes your common denominator. Every student is broke, from all levels. Some are broke because they've used up their own funds and they don't have access to more. Some are broke and they have access to more. Some are broke because they have angered their parents and a hold was put on their trust fund. Regardless, broke is the bottom line for most students. Thus, when you see an event that advertises free food, this means that you should be there 10 minutes before they even open the doors. Help set up the event if they'll let you. Get elected to an e-board to ensure that you can get the best food possible at those events.

So imagine in summer, my excitement for being invited to two, yes, two, conferences that featured free breakfast, lunch and dinner.

I am currently at the second of these events. For some reason, it occurred to me that I am here for much different reasons. Most of the people that are here are concerned solely about the topic at hand. Yeah, all the issues matter. But I'm hungry.

The problem with being this hungry in a group full of stuffed shirts is that sometimes, I forget the manners that I learned. It's not so much that I forget them so much as I am too focused on not being obvious that I make myself paranoid.

Of course, what adds to my paranoia is when I am not on the registration list. Now, this happened for both conferences. I think that the conference people must have reasoned that I am a student, I must be here primarily to save $10 from buying meals for myself, so it doesn't matter, if I don't have a name tag. Hey, you save, I save, we all save. Yeah!

But this conference slopped a big heap of insecurity onto my plate. It might have been the fact that I arrived at lunch and I couldn't find the people with whom I was supposed to sit. That five minute discomfort gave me a new perspective about this whole thing, and what was happening here.

The stuffed shirts were looking at me, wondering who or what dragged me into the luncheon. These are people that normally, as I say in my head, I would "skate right past," but in this moment, I am feeling a little vulnerable. I need them to let me feel ok while I attempt to maintain my dignity and effortlessly pilfer food while smiling and making small talk to hundreds. And after you realize that, there is this small moment when you feel like, was this worth the discomfort? Should I just work more so that I don't have to endure situations like these anymore?

And then your stomach rumbles, and you remember the urgency of this situation. This is good food, not some slop, leftovers from three days ago, or a bad of cholesterol from your favorite fast food chain. This is good, decent, recently cooked, professionally served food, with dishes that you can throw out (meaning that you don't have to wash any of them). There are people here on hand to clean up behind you. You don't have a lot of decent food, let alone food in general as an undergraduate, or as someone starting out on their own, and thus, you have to take good food when it's available. Right now, it won't matter if the president of the universe were looking at me, I would still be slopping a piece of chicken onto this plate, and looking for the free soda and roll and whatever else I can fit onto the plate, and that I can eat in one setting.

This makes me sound like I am a glutton. I really don't have a big appetite, but when you are trying to eat so that you won't be hungry for a few hours, a bizarre logic takes over that says that if you eat to your heart's content now, that contentment will assuage your hunger later.

So you take your food, sit at the table, listen to the speaker, and learn something hopefully along the way.

I did just that, and I was really elated to be able to have flan at this event. It seemed like the discomfort that happened a few minutes ago just melted away in the first spoonful. That was until I looked around the table. Everyone else had flan in this nice ceramic type container while I had been given the reject version in an aluminum circular thing. Did I even have a right to let this bother me? Not really, but I felt for a moment like I had been deemed not good enough to have what everyone else had.

I was distracted by the amusing things that were happening on stage. First of all, I misheard a bad orator. I was not sure that they had actually said words in any language, but what I made out from the garble was something about mistreatment by infants. The sheer thought of this caused me to laugh uncontrollably, inside my head. Laughing inside one's head is a skill to be mastered if you ever want to succeed in business. You have to keep a straight face but let all of your synapses and your blood vessels and cells laugh themselves into a frenzy which you will call a pleasant smile. This is what you have to do until you can get into the car with your friends and recall the stupidity that you experienced and laugh until you burst your appendix.

Added to this list was the sight of the sign language signer that was hired to translate at this event. The effortless bumbling of the speakers at this event gave the signer the worst time. It's bad enough when you can't hear someone, but then to also have to try to translate what you didn't even really hear and try to make it sound in some way feasible to a human mind can cause priceless facial demonstrations of frustration and confusion, as I witnessed at this event. I realized that she was also signing that the person had missed a word or said something inaudible. It was a combination of an on-the-spot speech revision and Mystery Science Theater.

These factors are what allowed me to get past the substandard container of my flan.

Really, though, whatever containers it's in, free flan is pretty darn good.

Chicken and Jeans

I have spoken before about the stress of not having money in college. This chapter is dedicated to the struggles and the crazy things that you do when in college.

This chapter was inspired by my thoughts when I was walking down the street, with no money in my pocket, with books in my bag that I was going to sell. As a student and someone that enjoys learning, should I not be saving these books and keeping them to refer to later on, and for my progeny? Well, that's very altruistic, and in a world where money is not necessary, then that would definitely work. When those books are worth money, and you have no money for lunch, you can choose to edify your mind or your body. A hungry man in 90 degree heat will definitely choose the latter. My heart literally sank when the guy at the college bookstore told me that they were not buying the books that I was bringing. Literally. My heart was actually in my shoe, which made walking kind of uncomfortable.

Access to money to college students is like crack to crack heads. I have never been this worried or concerned about money and I have never done this much to make sure that I have money. Although I said that I would never work in a fast food place, there I was at four in the morning working like a dog, with barbeque chicken sauce on my shirt, sweating like I had been on a treadmill for 10 hours, taking orders from the dredges of society. I have to say that I really liked the people that I worked with, my boss, and the cooks. It was the level of indecency to which I was exposed from the clientele that I didn't like.

Clientele is a word too important sounding to use in terms of the customers that came into that establishment. I never thought that I would ever get into an argument with someone over the price of bleu cheese, but it happened. I never thought that I would almost have to fight someone because I was closing the doors at the normal time, 3 AM (if that is a normal time) but it happened. The guy apparently was very hungry and viewed me as the greatest obstacle to the satisfaction of his palate. All of this because the place paid cash and I would always be able to have a discount on food.

That was definitely not my element.

Neither is chasing the dream of how many credit cards I can get people to sign up for at my local clothing retailer. Nor is hanging up clothes for 11 thousand hours until my fingertips are bleeding from the dryness of the corporate retail atmosphere. The worst thing that ever happened to the mall is when clothing chains decided to adopt corporate guidelines and regulations. Listen, I am only working at this store, let's call it Fissure, not because I am enamored with the lighting fixtures or the catchy commercials or the way that I look in your clothes. I am here solely because you hired me, I needed a job, and you offer me a discount on clothes that I most likely would not otherwise buy except for the fact that they are much cheaper since I work here, and I basically know before anyone else when things are going on sale. The reason that stores offer discounts to their employees is not because they love their employees. It is because most of their employees are some of their biggest customers. Look in the closet of anyone that has worked in a clothing store and you will see that most of their clothes are from that store. That's why they focus so much on getting discounts and special incentives for you to get low cost items all the time.

I am not however working at this store because I like the "culture" of this store. I am not here because I "believe in the product." I don't think that I am changing anyone's life or even making their day so much better by being here. I am here because I am poor. I would not have applied here if I had money and if I saw no immediate benefit from looking like an idiot with a name tag on my shirt, a shirt that was of course bought in your store.

What's worse is that they want you to start thinking like this is your life. They want to eat this store, breathe and bleed this store. They want you to be like your managers, who go to sleep staring at a picture of the founders of the company on their nightstand. They go to sleep in pajamas or worse yet, bedding, from the store to which they will return every day for the rest of their lives until someone wakes them up from the retail spell in which they live. It's scary when a grown person is upset with you because you are not smiling. This happens especially in the larger chains.

One manager said to an employee over the walkie-talkie something to the effect of, "Three people have come into your section and you have not said anything to them. We need for you to greet each customer that comes into the store."

Are you serious? So you want me to speak to 100 people during Christmas time? Half of those people don't want to talk to the people that they are with, let alone to some random stranger with a forced, "Please pretend for a second that I don't look constipated" smile on their face talking about, "Welcome to my store".

And then, they want you to push the latest items in their faces, remind them about sales, ask them if there is anything else that they want to buy, and ask them to sign up for a credit card. Plus, I worked in the fitting room at one store, so am I supposed to do all of that, and answer the phone, and remain sane?

Once, when I knew that the bitter end of my abysmal corporate retail experience was nigh, a customer gave me a pair of jeans that she had tried on, but that didn't work out for them. (By the way, it seemed standard operating procedure that we would ask them when they didn't take the clothes with them when they left, "So (emphasis on "so"), those didn't work out for you?" And then, we were supposed to ascertain what was wrong with that item and then suggest a solution.

Listen, a pair of jeans that is just too tight is just too tight. It's not like a relationship, something that needs to be salvaged and repaired. The customer will just try on another pair of jeans and like them or not like them, or leave the store before someone else tries to smile at them.

Anyway, as I am about to start folding the jeans in

the standard jeans folding style, I notice as I am folding that there is a wet stain in the crotch area. I noticed this because I felt something wet on my hand when I was folding these jeans. I contemplated for a moment what this wet stain could be, and decided to wave my finger in front of my face and get a whiff of what the stain was. After determining that someone mistook the fitting room for the rest room, I walked over to my manager, right next to the person who was at the counter buying another pair of jeans, that I had just experienced the most disgusting thing in my life. Touching the remains of someone else's is nearly as bad as the person's urinating on you. Yes, I endured all of this so that I could be able to pay $7 for a shirt.

Also in that store, I had all of the following things happen to me:

- I had 3 racks of hangers basically attack me by falling on my head when I bent down to pick up something.

- A customer threw a pair of jeans at me and the sensor tag struck me in the wrist, causing me intense pain and ire. (See the chapter titled "Ghetto" for details.)

- I was told that I could not answer the phone during the holiday season because I did not want to say "Happy Holidays." Apparently, I was supposed to be upset that I could not answer the phone during holidays. (Who wants to answer the phone during holidays at a store in the mall?)

- I had a customer ask me to put 12 pair of jeans on hold. They were all different sizes, styles and colors. She was serious.
- I had a grandmother from North Carolina call me in New Jersey to ask me to find a pair of chenille gloves for her infant granddaughter because she has been calling stores all over the East Coast for these gloves.

And through all of this I was supposed to keep my smile.

Here is a list of the wacky jobs that I have had while in college. They are in no particular order of chronology or importance. Some of them are not as crazy at the others, but keep in mind that this is over the course of five years that I had all of these jobs.

- Wood cutter, branch former, and styler at a silk tree factory
- Third Key Manager of a chicken fast food place
- Dispatcher for campus security
- Choreographer
- Server at school dining hall
- Summer camp counselor (I really liked this job)
- Market research for film companies
- Telemarketing (For two hours at one place, and then I tried it again for four hours at another place. It is hard to market alarms to someone

that you have reached at dinner time.)

- Intern (Prerequisite for a college student)
- Customer service at least four places
- Sales, at a home furnishings/plates and crap type place (I didn't even know what the purpose or the market of the store was until I quit.)
- Sales at a day planner store (I had to sit down with people and help them figure out which type of daily planner best suited their needs.)
- Teaching at a test prep company (Great job, except that they always got my checks wrong)
- One day working as the guy who decorates the edges of the plates at a fancy restaurant (it was too much for me to fathom that my job description would be plate decorator.)
- Operator at an alphanumeric pager company (twice, once on each side of the country.)

I'm sure that there are more, but isn't that enough? The things that we do to get paid.

I have an appointment to audition to teach dance on Monday.

Detox

Some relationships cost so much in time and effort. Some cost a lot in money. Some just are too emotionally expensive to afford.

I have just decided to let go of two of my priciest friendships.

There is always one or two persons in your circle of companions that is too costly to your emotions for your own good. They try you and again and again until you almost become used to the routine of listening or taking their crap. Their crap is usually about how they are mad at someone else in the group, how that person did them wrongly and the how much they are never going to hang out with or trust that person ever again.

And you listen.

You listen because you care. At first. Then after this becomes regular, you listen as if you care. You listen because you have no choice. There is no way to escape it. These conversations just come up on their own, and have a life of their own. They are like some type of parasite that feeds upon your inability to rip this person's tongue out of their head. This feeling is also aided into existence by conversations with the alleged bad friend. When this happens once, you tend to see both sides of the story. When it happens that everyone in the circle except for this person seems to see the situation the same way, this is when you start listening as if you care and not because you do. You realize that the names change in the story, but the plot and the outcome is always the same. What's even more interesting is that once everything is resolved with the alleged bad friend, or when someone else becomes the bad guy, then all of a sudden, the blame game switches.

Then you think about it and it becomes painfully obvious that you don't want to hear this story anymore. Ever again. Not even in its abridged form. You don't want to hear anyone tell this type of story ever again. As in, you don't want to hear this person tell any story anymore. And then this is also about the time, since this reprobate has had his or her problem with the whole group of friends, that it becomes your turn on the chopping block. Somehow in this moment, this person loses their minds, believing sincerely in their head that you really need them in your life.

This is when you can really embrace the term toxic in regards to friends .

Think of an appendix. Think of a big appendix (I am not sure how large appendices are, but just play along) filled with substances that might not kill a nation, but are definitely not supposed to be running rampantly through the body. Think of all of those toxins swelling to a point that a simple motion, a sneeze, a wink, a wrongly spoken syllable could cause it to rupture.

This is how it feels before the friend loses his mind.

Think of the hugest oil spill. Think of the worst disasters in history. Think liquid anger. Combine these three.

This is how it feels after the friend loses their mind.

This is the fallout that you feel after dealing with what this friend does or says to you when it is your time to be the bad guy. The funny thing is that everyone in the circle understands what is going on and feels for you. They are used to this and almost welcome you into the club of people that have had to deal with this toxic friend. It is like you are the last victim to enter the shelter after a natural disaster. Everyone before you knows what you are feeling and what you are going through.

The difference between you and them is that after hearing the same stories from the toxic friend over and over again, you really would rather not have the same story going around about you. It's not that you really care, but still, you don't really want to hear anything from anyone anyway about the situation. You don't want people to have to hear your name spoken with the same breath that this toxic friend breathes.

Then you realize that you either need some time off or a permanent vacation from this person. And then you do. I have had to look past the person as if they were not there, speak to them when they decide to speak. I have mastered this art although it is really hard. I am a nice person by nature, so it really pains me a little bit to have to ignore someone.

Then there is that breath of fresh air when you realize that you are free from this person's grapple hold. You can have conversations that have no relation to anything but something external to you and the other person(s) in the conversation. You can breathe easily when someone says that they have something to say to you, knowing that most likely, it's not going to be one of these awful complaints about life. It's amazing to remember that there is a whole world out there past bad talks with toxic people.

I enjoy detoxifying my life. It's like a mental massage.

Grow your Hair Long to Avoid the Cost of Haircuts

In college and being on one's own, you will come to know things like hunger, thirst and poverty more acutely than ever before and hopefully ever again.

This is my list of things I've done to deal with increasing needs and decreasing budgets.

Food

I've bought Maria cookies (3 for $1) and ate them for breakfast, lunch and dinner. I've also at times lived solely on tuna salad. Sometimes, I've even been creative and mixed everything possible into a tuna salad, including potatoes and eggs. I've spent days and nights existing off of peanut butter and jelly.

Twenty-five cent cookies are sometimes what saves me. There's a little store that sells fresh bagels that are fifty cents when it passes 9 PM. I have had spaghetti with just butter. There is also this stuff that my mom made that was basically arroz con leche, with rice, sugar, milk, cinnamon and if you are fortunate, vanilla flavoring. These are some solutions that even hunger won't allow.

In college, I have gone to the dining hall and taken home enough food to last for a lifetime for two people. I've made sandwiches and stuffed them in my bookbag. If I had Tupperware, pasta was coming home with me too.

Bills

Robbing Peter to pay Paul goes something like this. You pay a little bit on some bill so that you can have some type of payment history, so that they know that you aren't dead, and then you pay what you have to on your necessary bills. You pay your cell phone bill so that you can call people to go shower at their place when your water gets shut off for not paying the bill.

Hygiene and Grooming

Grooming is probably the funniest area when frugality is necessary for survival.

Grow your hair long to avoid haircuts. Call it rebellion or a phase that you are going through. It will save you $10 to $15 every other week.

Buying a 2-in-one shampoo and conditioner saves you a few bucks. It will make your hair a little stringy, but at least you know that it's clean. You can make that 2-in-1 into a 3-in-1 when you run out of soap and have to use it as "body wash" as well. Go for the gold. Make it 4-in-1 and use it for shaving cream. If you do buy the shampoo and conditioner separately, depending on your hair type, the conditioner can double as a light hair ointment.

You have to be clean, but you don't have to clean out the last dollar in your wallet to do so.

Your butt adjusts to 99 cent toilet paper after a while. You also learn to be conservative with your clothes. Remembering that jeans were not designed to be washed after each wear saves you more space in the washer for other clothes.

Fashion

White t-shirts and Clorox are of ultimate importance. They help mix up that five shirt, two jeans, one dress pants wardrobe that is so necessary. You can never go wrong with a t-shirt and a pair of jeans.

Colorful T-shirts with distinctive hats are good, cheap ways to get through a few days switching between a couple of pairs of jeans. People will notice your cool shirt and funky hat and not really pay attention to the rerun jeans.

This holds true with suits. Get one basic color — gray, black, beige, or olive. Then get a few shirts, give distinctive ties, and a pair of suspenders.

Follow this formula: Day 1, Full suit. Day 2, shirt, tie, and suit pants. Day 3, different shirt and tie with suit pants. Fourth day, bring back the full suit again with a bright shirt and cool tie, or basic shirt and bright tie.

End the week with a shirt, tie and suspenders combo with the suit pants, or if you have casual Friday, live it up and pull out those always wrinkled but supposedly "wrinkle-free" khakis. No one will ever notice that you have just one suit.

Yes, I have really mastered the art of being cheap. As an English major, this is all of the economics that I have ever needed to know.

Car-less in New Jersey

I know that there are many states in which it is very hard, nearly impossible, to not have a car. New Jersey is one of those states that makes it really tricky, because you need one and can't afford one at the same time. There is public transportation, but the farther that you are from New York, the less frequent and reliable this transportation is. I don't think that I have ever actually had a bus arrive on time in my city, or the surrounding city. It's always five minutes late here, five minutes early there, or someone decided to take a break. I understand that everyone is human and bus drivers have to have breaks as well, however, just for one's own sake, when you have a bus full of angry people that you have made late because you did not arrive on time, now might not be the time to take that timeout to eat your peanut butter sandwich.

Then there are the attitudes of the bus drivers. Sure, there are lots of people that get on a bus each day, and each of those people could each do something collectively that adds to completely piss off the driver. The problem with that is that one person will get the brunt of this anger, and for some reason, I have seen this more with bus drivers and DMV than I have seen with any other facet of existence. I would think that it would be harder to work in, say, a hospital – and besides, at least bus drivers (and DMV personnel) don't have to deal with blood and sickness on a daily basis.

Regardless, some of the attitudes are ridiculous. Once, at school, I was on a bus and this guy gets out of his seat to ask the bus driver something before his stop came up. He was asking about the route of the bus, because if the bus didn't turn at this one street, he would have to get out at the next stop. The poor guy asked the driver three times and the driver did not so much as blink. Finally, the guy asked, again very calmly, and the driver exploded as if the guy had not just asked him like 18 times for an answer. The driver started yelling the answer, saying, "Yes! Yes! Yes!!!"

This driver is also known to not pick up people that are clearing standing at a marked bus stop, and to completely ignore requests to stop at recognized stops. It reminds me of a combination of a bad horror film and Speed.

Taxis are another oddity that require consideration. In my area, the taxi picks up everyone and their mother. Literally. One time, I was in the cab going home. I was only traveling a distance of what should have been maybe five to seven minutes. First, the cab driver picks me up with a pregnant woman and her two already born children in the front seat, which apparently is not legal. Anyway, he goes to pick up this person and that person and soon, before I could say, "I'll just take the bus," there were literally 8 people in the cab.

When I lost it was when he picked up these guys that were going to a chess convention, who had flagged him down. They get in the cab and sit in the back where there are already two people (someone else and myself). Then one of them had the audacity to ask me to move over a little bit. I let him know that since the window lever was lodged into my thigh currently, unless he wanted me to stick my head out of the window, there was going to be no way that I could move over more. This pushed me over the edge, and I lost it on the driver as well. I told him, "Hey, there's someone over there walking. Why don't you pick him up, tie him to the roof and charge him half price? Or what about for two dollars, you can attach that other guy on the skateboard to the back bumper and tell him to hold on." Laughter ensued from everyone but the driver, who evidenced his feelings toward my comments by trying to back over me when I go to out of the cab.

A car is a necessary evil in New Jersey.

Writing this Book

This is like a mirror in a mirror, or one of those paintings within a painting. Writing this book is sometimes like therapy and sometimes like an obsession; I believe that it truly is a little bit of both. It's like catharsis and karma poised with carnival, all at the same time.

At times, it seems like everything is important to record and at the same time, nothing is that important. Not everything should be a chapter of my book. How do you know, though, the moments of your existence that define you enough to convey who you are and who you'd like to be considered? Who can make that determination?

This book is unstructured but regimented.

One person told me that this book reads the way that I talk, which is excellent because someone who doesn't know me should be able to ascertain how I am through reading this book.

I talk, therefore I am.

I'll see things that happen on a daily basis and forget to put them in my book. Then it becomes neurosis. Am I just writing about my life, or about life, or what? Or is it that I am writing about what is important to me, which is my life and what I do each day? I think it's more the second possibility. My life is a combination of the crazy things that have happened to me, and how I react to them.

So maybe not everything should be a chapter, but all of these things that add to the chapters of my life.

Other Little Things to Know About Me

This is a list of random things about me that don't really deserve a chapter, but that you should know if you plan to ever understand me.

I used to work with the wife of Bozo the Clown. She was not very funny herself.

I am allergic to aluminum, dust, spores, mold, dairy products, pears, and most detergents.

I have eyes with very large curvatures.

I got locked in an ATM lobby outside of a bank at about 12:30 AM and had to use a pen to force the door open so that I could exit.

I was born on the same day as Whitney Houston, and International Indigenous People's Day.

I love the smell of gasoline.

I think that Hello Kitty is hilarious, as I have mentioned before (but it bears repeating), since she has no mouth.

I always wanted a Yugo or a Renault Alliance or a Jeep anything when I was growing up.

I don't like water being sprayed at my face. It makes me feel like I am a bad cat. (You can use water to train a cat to let them know that they have done something wrong. You spray them with the water when they err.)

I wanted a hamster when I was younger. My mother told me to wait until I was 18. I told her that I would probably not want one then. She told me that this was exactly her point.

I had one of my paintings sold at an auction in New York.

I am sure that there are more little things that you should know. I'll save them for the next book.

About Christopher J. Paige

Christopher Paige has been dancing since childhood. He's competed in closed circuit and open ballroom and Latin dance competitions throughout the United States. He has appeared on MTV and ABC (Good Morning America). He has 16 years of experience as an instructor and choreographer at Arthur Murray Dance Studios, four years as Coach of the Rutgers University Salsa Team, and is a Zumba instructor.

He maintains active participation in the dance community, including Ballroom for Seniors, and as a volunteer coach for youth dance teams in New York City.

He has worked for Yelp, Signpost, AppCard and other digital/internet based advertising and marketing companies, as well as a career in Fitness/Training Sales at New York Sports Club and LA Fitness.

Christopher is the author of "Redefining Masculinity" and the soon-to-be-released "Brown in this Town." As a writer, Christopher has been writing as a hobby since childhood, throughout college, up to the present. The last few years, and the pandemic, have sparked his foray into podcasting and blogging to bring his unique life experience and perspective to the world.

www.christopherjpaige.nyc

About Green Heart Living

Green Heart Living's mission is to make the world a more loving and peaceful place, one person at a time. Green Heart Living Press publishes inspirational books and stories of transformation, making the world a more loving and peaceful place, one book at a time.

Whether you have an idea for an inspirational book and want support through the writing process – or your book is already written and you are looking for a publishing path – Green Heart Living can help you get your book out into the world.

You can meet Green Heart authors on the Green Heart Living YouTube channel and the Green Heart Living Podcast.

www.greenheartliving.com

www.ingramcontent.com/pod-product-compliance
Lightning Source LLC
Chambersburg PA
CBHW062112080426
42734CB00012B/2838